AND HE SHALL BE CALLED

ADVOCATE—LAMB OF GOD
1 John 2:1   John 1:29

SHEPHERD & BISHOP OF SOULS—JUDGE
1 Peter 2:25   Acts 10:42

LORD OF LORDS—MAN OF SORROWS
1 Timothy 6:15   Isaiah 53:3

HEAD OF THE CHURCH—MASTER
Ephesians 5:23   Matthew 8:19

FAITHFUL & TRUE WITNESS—ROCK
Revelation 3::14   1 Corinthians 10:4

HIGH PRIEST—THE DOOR—LIVING STONE
Hebrews 6:20   John 10:9   John 4:10

BREAD OF LIFE—ROSE OF SHARON
John 6:35   Song of Solomon 2:1

ALPHA & OMEGA—TRUE VINE—MESSIAH
Revelation 22:13   John 15:1   Daniel 9:25

TEACHER—HOLY ONE—MEDIATOR
John 3:2   Mark 1:24   1 Timothy 2:5

THE BELOVED—BRANCH—CARPENTER
Ephesians 1:6   Isaiah 11:1   Mark 6:3

GOOD SHEPHERD—LIGHT OF THE WORLD
John 10:11   John 8:12

IMAGE OF THE INVISIBLE GOD—THE WORD
Colossians 1:15   John 8:12

CHIEF CORNERSTONE—SAVIOR—SERVANT
Ephesians 2:20   John 4:20   Matthew 12:18

AUTHOR & FINISHER OF OUR FAITH
Hebrews 12:2

THE ALMIGHTY—EVERLASTING FATHER
Revelation 1:8   Isaiah 9:6

SHILOH—LION OGF THE TRIBE OF JUDAH
Genesis 49:10   Revelation 5:5

I AM—KING OF KINGS—PRINCE OF PEACE
John 8:58   1 Timothy 6:15   Isaiah 9:6

BRIDEGROOM—ONLY BEGOTTEN SON
Matthew 9:15   John 3:16

WONDERFUL COUNSELOR—IMMANUEL
Isaiah 9:6   Matthew 1:23

SON OF MAN—DAYSPRING—THE AMEN
Matthew 20:28   Luke 1:78   Revelation 3:14

KING OF THE JEWS—PROPHET—REDEEMER
Mark 15:26   Matthew 21:11   Job 19:25

ANCHOR—BRIGHT MORNING STAR
Hebrews 6:19   Revelation 22:16

THE WAY, THE TRUTH & THE LIFE
John 14:6

JESUS CHRIST

OTHER BOOKS BY JAY R. LEACH

How Should We Then Live

Behold the Man

The Blood Runs Through It

Drawn Away

GIVE
ME
JESUS

Embracing the Man
Who is the Authentic Christ

JAY R. LEACH

Order this book online at www.trafford.com
or email orders@trafford.com

Most Trafford titles are also available at major online book retailers.

Unless otherwise indicated, Scripture quotations are from the New King
James Version, 2007 by Thomas Nelson, Inc. Nashville, TN

Printed in the United States of America.

ISBN: 978-1-4669-8846-0 (sc)
ISBN: 978-1-4669-8845-3 (e)

Trafford rev. 04/04/2013

 www.trafford.com

North America & international
toll-free: 1 888 232 4444 (USA & Canada)
phone: 250 383 6864 ♦ fax: 812 355 4082

ON THIS OUR FIFTIETH WEDDING
ANNIVERSARY, I DEDICATE THIS BOOK
TO MY WIFE, MAGDALENE,
YOUR LOVE HAS BEEN THE GREATEST
SUSTAINING HUMAN INFLUENCE IN MY LIFE.

WORKING UP TO "GIVE ME JESUS" EXPLAINED

For years the state of the church in America has been an increasing concern due to its growing irrelevance to many of the communities in which the churches are located. Research reveals that Christianity in the United States has become more and more distorted and less like Christ with each passing generation. A biblical world view based on absolute truth has been all but eliminated from the national view. The last three years of my life have been devoted to an agonizing review of the impact of the postmodern and post-Christian culture on the local church.

There seem to be a growing voluntary institutional ignorance toward the two! This ignorance falls right at the feet of those of us whom Christ has mandated to "make disciples." How? Through the power of the Gospel of Jesus Christ manifested through us as His counter to the culture. However it seems that much of the American church has bowed to the mandates of the culture. Is the culture's secular worldview replacing the church's biblical worldview forged by the truths of God's Word? Through our "voluntary silence," we have failed to pass on the mantel (of life and the mandate of Christ) to the next generation in the church; which has produced a growing disparity in intergenerational dialogue.

The presence of the Holy Spirit is the *common denominator*. When concerned Christians believe in and support the ongoing work of the Holy Spirit in the Church, the body of Christ, will find unity. The church must allow the Holy Spirit's power to grow today as happened in the early church. When the Church grows in the Holy Spirit, the saints' lives bear the fruit of the Spirit (see Galatians 5:22-23) and the manifestation of Christ in their corporate as well as individual lives. Then the Spirit will draw people to Christ through His manifested life in us. We must realize that the first fruit of the Spirit is love:

Speaking the truth in love, I was privileged to write *How Should We then Live,* about the need of every Christian, and especially church leaders, to devote time to understanding our culture in conjunction with the unique mandate Christ has given His Church "to make disciples."

In *Behold the Man,* as depressing as conditions may appear in some areas, Christ Jesus is among humanity today incarnate in ordinary Christians energizing our spirits through the truth of God's Word and the power of the Holy Spirit, carrying out His mission in the world.

Too many pastors in America today are bowing to Satan's deception that says "there are many ways to God." prominent people in every quarter are spouting this error. In my book *The Blood Runs through It,* humanity is in a predicament with no possible way out without Divine intervention. God's remedy demanded the blood of Jesus, His Son in our stead. Sin caused alienation and separation from a Holy God, and made it impossible for humans in their sinful state to stand in His presence. Jesus said of Himself, *"I am the way, the truth, and the life. No one comes to the Father except through Me"* (John 14:6).

Cultural influence in the church is running rampart in America; each day more and more congregations bow to the new tolerance and relativism which demands a clear change of the biblical worldview and adoption of the hedonistic secular view. Many have been *Drawn Away* from absolute truth through this new thought running rampart throughout the culture and endorsed by secular academia. During His time on earth Jesus modeled for us, how to live a victorious life through His confrontation with Satan (see

Matthew 4:1-11). He defeated him through two strategies which He has passed on to His followers:

- He demonstrated throughout His life that He lived to please God.
- He defeated Satan through dependence on the Holy Spirit and the spoken Word of God.

Praise God, He made the same actions and authority available to all believers corporately and individually. With all the activity of the spin doctors, the dismal news from the media, opinions and other sources have left people confused and everywhere wondering, "Whose report shall I believe?" Over the past century the church has forfeited the fate of the people to the whims of the culture and wider society; which is 180 degrees in the opposite direction of God's plan. The failures of this experience have choked intergenerational dialogue, leaving a generation of young people and a generation of seniors in distrust on "shaky ground," feeling that they have to fend for themselves. They desire the authentic Christ of the Gospels, who connects people with God not the Jesus conjured up by the culture of the day. "What's next?" There is hope! We must embrace Jesus, the Authentic Christ, *"Give Me Jesus!"*

INTRODUCTION

Every religion has its own story comprising specific beliefs and characteristics that makes it unique from all others. The Thorndike Barnes dictionary defines religion as a particular system of religious beliefs and worship of God or gods. Another observation concerning religion is the fact that it is external and cultural. [For example, the use of dress codes, hair styles, laws and traditions]. Brackets are mine throughout.

The United States and much of the Western world are undergoing a total transformation of their societies today. I'm not sure that we are aware of the incredible negative affect multicultural, post modern and post Christian attitudes are having on that change. Our own national life and thought over the past three or four decades has done an about face on God. In the mind of the world, Christianity is equated with Western culture; the current anti-Western wave discredits our traditional Christian beliefs, values and biblical worldview right along with the culture. The Holy Spirit can adapt biblical faith to any culture. But because of American greed, materialism, secularism, and multiculturalism all of which flow from sinful human nature, the biblical God and absolute truth are fast becoming null and void to many who know better across this nation and the world.

True Christianity is unique to religion in that it is *exclusive*, "You must be born again," (John 3:3; 1 Corinthians 15:44-48). It dares not to be inclusive as main stream America and many religions demand. For example, *Chrislam which says, an individual neither "converts" nor turns from their previous religion. The individual simply claims Jesus as Lord, and therefore, becomes a religious **dual** citizen.*[1] In its role in the world as salt and light; the church must be counter-cultural in obedience to the Word of God.

Unlike the various religions, overloaded with traditional belief systems full of dead founders and laws; Christianity is more than a system of beliefs. It is a life [in Christ], with a Founder who is alive and *dwelling within* His followers. No religion has that claim. Yet! Knowing this to be true as a people we are turning our backs on Christ in the most blessed nation in the world. At a very fast pace the gospel is being intellectualized and redefined to such an extent [the word "gospel" today is thought of more as a "music style"] than "the power of God unto salvation."

Additionally, there is little or no mention of true faith, nor the need to trust Jesus Christ, and His many promises of abundant life. Therefore, His mandate to "make disciples" of all nations is also going unheeded or unknown in many local churches. Academic achievements and speaking ability are held in high esteem while spiritual maturity, character, being Spirit-formed, and manifesting the fruit of the Spirit are relegated to little or no importance. They are treated as being irrelevant or antiquated in church work and the work of the church. Grasping such a position is totally ungodly. The absence of true confession, repentance [turn-a-round], and commitment is inviting the wrath of Almighty God upon this nation. No matter what humanity thinks, Almighty God is God over the secular as well as the sacred. This was the one nation truly blessed of God for its biblical worldview. It was founded under the God of Abraham, Isaac, and Jacob, who's virgin-born Son died for the sins of the whole world.

I believe the god of this world is making inroads through a highly recognized worldly system of deception known as multiculturalism [with its many imported gods and religions]. This belief system trains its students to view the world and its people from a global and pantheistic perspective rather than from a national and Judeo-Christian perspective. This clash of religions and Christianity has placed a tension between the world and the authentic Word of God. In other words, it is designed to speed the paradigm shift through transformation toward a radical new way of thinking, believing, and relating to our so-called inclusive "global family." Satan is putting forth a great effort to diffuse Christianity through high-tech superhighways and a common set of secular values.

Tragically he has been able to dupe many of our foundational institutions especially the governmental and educational systems; which in turn are affecting the local churches and redefining our critical cultural-building blocks of marriage and the family. The aim of multiculturalism is to mold cosmopolitan world-class citizens. It is constantly reported in the media that social engineers are testing the latest techniques in behavior modification on our children. Our society has reached the point where children must either reject their old church and home-taught faith or stretch it far beyond the limits of a viable biblical worldview in order to accommodate the world's pantheistic [equates God with the forces and laws of the universe], polytheistic [belief or worship of more than one god]; which requires the total abandonment of the authentic Jesus Christ. Listen to words shared to a graduating class of Hampden-Sydney College:

It is a serious step, in these days, even from the worldly point of view to become a Christian. There was a time, not so very long ago, when the faithful Christian was supported by public opinion or at least by the united opinion of the visible church. But that time has gone by. The man who today enters upon the Christian life is enlisting in a warfare against the whole current of the age.[2]

This exert from a graduation speech made by Christian theologian J. Gresham Machen in 1929. Spoken 84 years ago, and it seems brought to fruition in the past 14 years. All remnants of our nation's Christian underpinning are being removed without little notice it seems from the Christian church. It seems as the old "Gung Ho" generations of the World War II and prior grow smaller and smaller so goes the thoughtful Christian influence. This lack of influence is accompanied by exclusion of Christianity from the public square. This abandonment is encouraging an individualized, privatized, eclectic unscriptural faith among many professing Christians today. These men and women in action and attitude are helping the negative version of Christianity forged by secular society, and does not have the authentic Christ as its Head. While the church fiddles the young people are distancing themselves further and further from this non-spiritual façade parading as the church today. Now that Satan has forced many local churches to remain inside the four walls, he has intensified his efforts to discredit the truth of God's Word. "Did God say?"

The emerging generation of Christians seems to have lost any solid understanding of true Christianity. This loss began with their great grandparents as passed down from generation to generation. As a result, too many professing Christians to include many church leaders no longer have a real clear understanding of who God is or how they are to relate to Him. This is seen very clearly in their daily lives and personal decisions. Like the world, they have set God aside as an irrelevant being out there [somewhere?].

It is imperative that the Christian community facilitate a deeper, more authentic vision of the Christian faith in our pluralistic culture. The Christian leadership must join together and strive for the promotion of a biblical worldview beginning by embracing God's story [the authentic Christ], with intergenerational dialogue; at the same time engaging parents, families, extended family members, and other guardians with relevant information, skills, and tools. This provides opportunities that will encourage and empower them for community advancement and service.

Because of the demands of true Christianity, many individuals and churches compromise the "truth" of God's Word. Unless the churches [the true salt and light Christians] wake up and make a difference; these various encroaching errors through government, education and other secular agencies will soon be enabled to completely control Christians in the home and the local church. Remember, the secularly-controlled school systems has access to our children for more than thirty-five hours a week and are seeking more, for their indoctrination as compared to the church's forty-five minutes to a couple of hours at best once a week! Recently I heard a reputable pollster on TBN state that statistics show more people are being born-again worldwide today; than are being born through natural birth. I don't know whether that's a fair assessment or not, but I do know there is a great move of God going on around the world. If you'll notice slowly but surely the children of the Christian converts of our foreign missionaries of yester-year are flooding the airwaves of Christian television especially in America and the West striving to convert us to Christianity. Sad to say America has become one of the largest missionary opportunities in the world. I read a statistic that stated, if the unsaved in America was separated into a country it would be the fifth largest country in the world.

My wife and I personally experienced that move in Central America in the 70's as we were fully engaged with the Church of God while stationed there in the U.S. Army for three years; and we witnessed the same while stationed two years in Seoul, Korea in the 80's. A check of research on the subject today reveals report after report containing the results of the great movement of God on going today in South America, Africa, China and many other emerging nations. It's amazing how the Apostle Paul, the apostle to the Gentiles set out from Antioch under the guidance of the Holy Spirit carried the gospel into Europe and to the world. Through the years the gospel has moved from there around the world and it seems to be moving mightily again in the Middle East, in spite of all of the on going turmoil there. I believe the gospel is poised for the last mighty push there in these last days. Nothing is too hard for God!

I envision Satan struggling overtime trying a counter attack. Notice the on going efforts to make Europe Christ-less and over the past 50 years there has been a rapid downward spiral of moral values and loss of virtues here in the United States. In 1962 the U.S. Supreme Court issued a decision to remove prayer from the schools; opening the doors for a host of evil demons to invade this entire country. An entire generation was made vulnerable to this horde. From that time until the present, a process of changing America's fundamental institutions has been firmly implanted in the hearts and attitudes of much of the American population. Satan's agenda has continuously pressed for a "new norm," a Christ-less society. Each decade since the 60's has been marked by anti-biblical decisions at the highest levels of leadership in the church and state that further puts this nation at odds with a Holy God. *The wicked shall be turned into hell and all the nations that forget God" (Psalm 9:17).* There's an old saying, "If you think education is expensive, try ignorance!" Resistance to change has set many churches against the Spirit's counter movement. Perhaps, as Jesus said on the cross, "They do not know what they are doing." Many of Christianity's leaders simply believed the propaganda and have joined the systematic movement they do not understand. Our only hope in countering Satan's societal initiatives is the authentic Jesus Christ working through His own truly blood-washed, Bible believing, spiritually mature disciples. Jesus trained and engaged 12 men, who through that training and His presence in them turned the world upside down. Give me Jesus!

Albert Einstein has been credited with the comment, "the kind of *thinking* that will solve the world's problems will be of a different order to the kind of *thinking* that created those problems in the first place." I remember sitting at my computer on the night of [September 13, 2012] working on the manuscript of this book; pondering the unrest in the Middle East and the tragic loss of our Ambassador and three other Americans, as the most powerful man in the world attended a re-election fundraiser. Politician after politician publicly scolded him in the media that night because he was not physically in the White House. Undoubtedly delegation of authority works for him?

Delegation of spiritual authority through Spiritual gifts in Spirit-filled people must occupy top priority on the church leaders' lists of changes if our communities of faith are to remain viable parts of the authentic body of Christ. Little more than a decade into the third millennium, many local churches are in deep trouble. Why? They chose to *mingle* their biblical theology with cultural influences and the religious practices of others over authentic Christianity. Daily we hear such phrases as "post-Christian era" and "Some denominations are debating the deletion of being "born again" as a requirement for getting to heaven." Definitely many churches are using these criteria for church membership in spite of Christ's command (see John 3:3). Contrast those comments with these assessments made by the world concerning the early church:

- Believers were first called Christian [little Christ (s)] at Antioch because of their Christlikeness.
- "Oh, how those Christians love one another," was historically expressed by a period historian during the early church era.

In the ensuing chapters we will consider God's story and plan for humanity who by choice sinned and alienated himself from his Creator, God. In each chapter we will consider the distinguishing characteristics of God's eternal *plan of regeneration and reconciliation*; which He had in place for mankind from the foundation of the world. He reached down to lost humans with His One and only solution to their impossible predicament—the authentic Jesus Christ! God came down to us! The people of the various religions have failed or refused to grasp these truths; and simply continue their so-called journey depending on their own efforts to reach up to God through soulish endeavors; which in many respects create their own image of Christ, actually anti-Christ. Jesus remains the *only* authentic answer to the world's woes, and He is fully engaged through His blood-washed, spiritually mature disciples in Christ; who are scattered throughout the world at all levels of societies and operating in the cultures as salt making life for others more palatable and being moons reflecting the light of the Son of God, guiding lost souls from the kingdom of darkness into the kingdom of light. *Give me Jesus,* the authentic Christ! At the end of each chapter, you'll find some very practical questions with answers to help you move the truths expressed in this book to life application. Please contact us through our e-mail, bolm@ embarqmail.com or website www.breadoflifenc.com if you need help with the questions or any part of this work.

Jay R. Leach
Fayetteville, North Carolina

CONTENTS

SECTION I—GOD'S ETERNAL STORY

SECTION II—THE AUTHENTIC CHRIST

SECTION III—SALVATION IN NO OTHER

SECTION IV—GIVE ME JESUS

SECTION V—THE GOSPEL (CHRIST)

SECTION I

God's Eternal Story

Chapter 1

GOD'S STORY IN CREATION

Several thousand years ago Moses, under the inspiration of the Holy Spirit wrote, *"In the beginning God created the heavens and the earth"* (Genesis 1:1). These are the first words of the Bible, and they are the most logical and satisfactory explanation ever given of the origin of the universe.

The Bible begins with a living, all-powerful, all-wise God, who has the power to create or to make things out of nothing. He is presented as the great Architect and Builder of all things. *"By him were all things created, that are in heaven, and that are in earth, visible and invisible, whether they be thrones, or dominions, or principalities, or powers; all things were created by him, and for him: and he is before all things, and by him all things consist"* (Colossians 1:16, 17).

Created by God

And, *"You Lord, in the beginning laid the foundation of the earth, and the heavens are the work of Your hands"* (Hebrews 1:10). God's story beginning with the creation as found in the first three chapters of Genesis declares that the earth, and all that pertains to it, was made in six days, perfect and good (see Genesis 1:31; 2:1).

Everything started in its creation at its highest state of perfection. The first lily that bloomed on the earth was not evolved from some wild plant, but, on the very day that it was created, it shined forth in glory greater than Solomon's. The grapes hung in full, delicious clusters on the vine. The giant trees of the forests were perfect in form and size on the day that they were created.

"These are the generations of the heavens and the earth when they were created, in the day that the Lord God made the earth and the heavens, and every plant of the field before it was in the earth, and every herb of the field before it grew" (Genesis 2:4, 5).

And God said, *"Behold, I have given you every herb bearing seed, which is upon the face of all the earth, and every tree, in which is the fruit of the tree yielding seed; and to you it shall be for meat"* (Genesis 1:29).

Therefore, these things did not grow up by slow development from atoms or some glob. Everything in the world and the universe whether man, animal, or plant started with a full-grown and perfect life. That is God's Creation. The idea that it all began with a big bang or evolved from some lower species is a lie concocted by Satan, God's enemy. The evolutionist knows of no beginning. If he or she thinks back to a time when there was nothing, then they've traveled too far, since he or she has nothing to begin with and no one to plan a beginning. That person is always groping in the dark.

The most perfect human being, aside from Christ, ever to live upon the earth was the first man. He was like God. The Scripture says, *"So God created man in his own image, in the image of God created he him; male and female created he them"* (Genesis 1:17). Man was God's masterpiece in the creation of the earth. He was to have been God's personal representative and to govern in His new creation. It's so sad that man should ever have fallen from that high estate and forfeited his right even to his home in Eden!

An angel rebels

"You were perfect in your ways from the day
You were created, till iniquity was found in you"
(Ezekiel 28:15).

Back in the distant past, before the creation of the earth there was among the mighty angels of God one "Lucifer," who was known as the "son of the morning." He held the exalted position of leader of the angelic choir and stood next to the Son of God in command of the heavenly host. The Bible records how this exalted being finally organized a rebellion against God, led a host of angels to follow him and was later expelled from heaven. This Lucifer now transformed into "the devil," has become the sworn enemy of God and all those who seek to follow Him. Satan is not your friend!

The Bible's record of this lawlessness in heaven is astonishing. The Apostle John declares, *"And war broke out in heaven: Michael and his angels fought with the dragon; and the dragon fought and his angels, but they did not prevail, nor was there place found for them in heaven any longer. So the great dragon was cast out, that serpent of old, called the Devil, and Satan, who deceives the whole world: he was cast to the earth, and his angels were cast out with him"* (see Revelation 12:7-9).

So Satan came from heaven. Jesus declared, *"I beheld Satan as lightening fall from heaven"* (Luke 10:18). The mighty Lucifer was one of God's created beings. He was not the Creator, nor was he in any sense equal to God the Father or His Son; but because of his exalted position and the beauty and perfection of his person, he became lifted up, and jealousy filled his heart. That was the beginning of his downfall. Ezekiel left us the following record of Lucifer's fall under the name of the Prince of Tyre.

*"Son of man, take up a lamentation upon the king of Tyre, and say to him, "Thus says the Lord God: "You were the seal of perfection, full of wisdom and perfect in beauty. You were in Eden the garden of God; every precious stone was your covering, the sardius, topaz, and diamond, beryl, onyx, jasper, sapphire, turquoise, and emerald with gold: the workmanship of your timbrels and pipes was prepared for you on the day you were created. You **were** the anointed cherub who covers; I established you: You were on the holy mountain of God; you walked back and forth in the midst of fiery stones. **You were perfect** in your ways from the day you were created, **till iniquity was found in you.** By the abundance of your trading you became filled with violence*

*within, and you sinned. Therefore **I cast you** as a profane thing **out of the mountain of God;** and I destroyed you, O covering cherub, from the midst of the fiery stones. Your heart was lifted up because of your beauty; you corrupted your wisdom for the sake of your splendor; I cast you to the ground, I laid you before kings that they might gaze at you."* (Ezekiel 28:11-17).

Not Created a Devil

The fact that Lucifer was created is evidence that he is not equal to the great self-existent God, but he was not created a devil. **He was perfect.** God had made him so. There was no root of sin or iniquity in him. But it was with him that sin originated. God was in no way responsible for his downfall. Created with a free-will, Lucifer had the same power to do right as did any of the other created beings in God's universe.

There was no legitimate excuse for his disaffection and subsequent transgression; the chief reasons given in the Bible for the disaffection of Lucifer are pride and jealousy. Jesus later declared of him that he was a liar and the **father of lies.** That is, sin had its origin or beginning in the heart of this angel, and for it God had absolutely no responsibility. *"Your heart was lifted up because of your beauty; you corrupted your wisdom for the sake of your splendor; I cast you to the ground, I laid you before kings that they might gaze at you"* (Ezekiel 28:17).

The working of Lucifer's mind at that time is clearly described by the prophet Isaiah:

"How you are fallen from heaven,
O Lucifer, son of the morning!
How you are cut down to the
Ground,
You who weakened the nations!
For you have said in your heart:
I will ascend into heaven,

I will exalt my throne above the
Stars of God;
I will also sit on the mount of the
Congregation,
On the farthest sides of the north;
I will ascend above the heights of
The clouds,
I will be like the Most High.
Yet you shall be brought down to
Sheol,
To the lowest depths of the pit"
(Isaiah 14:12-14).

We can see that, Lucifer was determined to be no longer numbered among the angels. Therefore, he would establish his rule over the angelic host and even displace God Himself. This rebellion against God and His kingdom was sin. The apostle John declares, "Sin is transgression of the law" (see 1 John 3:4). Lucifer now regarded himself no longer accountable to God's rule.

The rebellion of Lucifer produced a great change. He began at once to seek the support of the angels. This rebellion was completely unsuccessful. The Bible declares that Satan and his angels were defeated in the conflict; and were cast out of heaven. *"God did not spare the angels who sinned, but cast them down to hell and delivered them into chains of darkness, to be reserved for judgment"* (2 Peter 2:4).

God could have destroyed Satan and his demons immediately, but it would have inspired fear in the hearts of all God's creatures, and they would have served Him thereafter only because they dared not do otherwise. They would have been no better than robots. This would have brought no glory to God, and His kingdom would stand on an unstable foundation. His creatures must be able to decide of their own volition, whether they desire to continue to *stand with God and truth* or whether they too, wish to enlist under the banner of Satan. The choice must rest with each individual. Satan has not given up to this day hoping to regain his position in heaven and extend his influence throughout the universe.

The Tempter in Eden

After the earth was created and man was placed upon it, Satan made his appearance in the Garden of Eden with the express purpose of leading man to join him in his rebellious agenda. With subtlety and guile he approached the human inhabitants of Eden. He did not appear in person, but chose the then beautiful serpent as his medium.

God had placed in the midst of the trees of the Garden one tree that was to serve as a test of man's loyalty to Him. The tree was designated "the tree of the knowledge of good and evil." Man had been given free access to all the other trees of the garden. God had provided more than their every need; therefore no hardship was imposed upon Adam and Eve when God said, ***"But of the tree of the knowledge of good and evil you shall not eat, for in the day that you eat of it you shall surely die."*** By obeying and not partaking of the fruit of this tree, man showed his reverence for God and recognized His ownership and control over Eden and all the earth.

Watching for an opportunity, the tempter caught Eve at the right moment as she gazed upon this forbidden tree. Suddenly a melodious voice was heard speaking to her from the tree saying, *"Has God indeed said, 'You shall not eat of every tree of the garden?"* Now that he had arrested her attention, [as if to say, "God is holding out on you"] he immediately led her into the great temptation to risk an act of disobedience to her Creator. Falling for Satan's deception, *[which remains his primary tactic to this day]* they ate of the forbidden tree [Read Genesis 3:2-7 for the disastrous outcome].

This is the saddest story ever told. It is the record, not merely of what happened to Adam and Eve in the Garden of Eden, but of a tragic predicament that produced the transmission of original sin or depravity and death to the entire unborn human race. All succeeding generations have suffered untold miseries as a result of it. By this rebellious and disobedient act by Adam and Eve, the heads of the human race, the entire course of human history was tragically changed:

- Man had *chosen* a new leader.
- He had *disobeyed God* and followed the counsel of God's enemy.
- By joining the rebel leader, he had *cut himself off* from God's protection and care.
- He *must now* suffer the consequences.

Hiding from God

Following the experience of eating the forbidden fruit, the Lord visited Eden in the cool of the evening and called Adam and Eve. But now they were ashamed with hearts full of remorse. Their consciences were heavily burdened with guilt, and they were afraid to meet Him:

- Whose love and tender care they had disregarded.
- For the first time they had become *self-conscious* of their nakedness.
- To supply *their own lack,* they made aprons of fig leaves which they sewed together. They now considered themselves to be self-reliant.

How could they appear before God? Covered with shame and filled with fright lest they be instantly destroyed by the power of their Maker, they "hid themselves from the presence of God among the trees of the garden" (see Genesis 3:8).

"Then the Lord God called to Adam and said to him, "Where are you?" So he said, "I heard Your voice in the garden, and I was afraid because I was naked, and I hid myself." And He said,

"Who told you that you were naked? Have you eaten from the tree of which I commanded you that you should not eat?" (Genesis 3:9-11).

Forced now to make a confession, both Adam and Eve add to their guilt as they seek to escape full responsibility for their transgression by casting the blame upon others. The man said, "The woman whom you gave to be with me, she gave me of the tree, and I ate." *[Adam blames both God and his own wife Eve].* And the Lord God said to the woman, "What is this you have done?" The woman said, "The serpent deceived me, and I ate" (verse 12). *[When Eve was questioned as to her part in the transgression, she followed her husband's example]. And the woman said, "The serpent deceived me, and I ate"* (verse 13).

Adam's sin was evidenced by his new knowledge of the evil of nakedness, but God still waited for Adam to *confess* to what He knew they had done. The basic reluctance of sinful people to admit their iniquity is here established. *Repentance* is still the issue. When sinners refuse to repent, they suffer judgment and when they do repent they receive forgiveness.

The Wages of Sin

The guilt of their sin could not be shifted so easily. It was very clearly theirs. God's warning to them had been clear and direct, ***"but of the tree of the knowledge of good and evil you shall not eat, for in the day that you eat of it you shall surely die"*** (Genesis 2:17). They were therefore without excuse. What they had done was done deliberately. From that time on they would be subject to decay and death; they had forfeited their hold on life. Now they must suffer the consequences (Read Genesis 3:14-19).

You will notice God cursed the serpent and the ground, but be thankful He did not curse Adam and Eve. Notice after God cursed the physical serpent; He turned to the spiritual serpent, Satan and cursed him:

"And I will put enmity
Between you and the woman,
And between your seed and her Seed;
He shall bruise your head
And you shall bruise His heel"
(Genesis 3:15).

This "first gospel" is prophetic of the struggle and its outcome between "your seed" [Satan and unbelievers, called his children in John 8:44] and her seed [Christ, a descendent of Eve, and those "in Him"] which began in the garden. In the midst of the curse passage, a message of hope lights the way, the woman's seed called "He" is Christ who will one day defeat the Serpent. Satan could only "bruise" Christ's heel (cause Him to suffer), while Christ will bruise Satan's head (deliver the fatal blow).

A Second Chance

If God had not added love and mercy with justice, Adam and Eve would have suffered death immediately following their sin. Though the first physical deaths should have been Adam and Eve; it was an animal. God shed the animal's blood to make tunics of skin, and clothed them (see v. 21). This is a shadow of the reality that God would someday kill a substitute to redeem sinners. God had a plan laid out by which He would make redemption possible for fallen humankind. In time the plan would be fully revealed to the fallen race; He would give them another chance!

STUDY SUMMARY

CHAPTER 1

GOD'S STORY IN CREATION

Is there really a devil?

"Be sober; be vigilant, because your adversary the devil walks about like a roaring lion, seeking whom he may devour" (see 1 Peter 5:8).

Was Satan always a devil?

No, he originally was one of God's highest angels in heaven. God had created him to be the "anointed cherub" to stand by God's throne and cover it with his outstretched wings. He was very beautiful, full of wisdom, and a skillful musician. He was perfect in all his ways. (see Ezekiel 28:12-15; 26:13).

What changed this beautiful angel into the devil?

Rebellion and sin changed this angel. He became proud because of his beauty. (see Ezekiel 28:15-17). He became jealous of God and determined to take His place as Ruler of the universe. (see Isaiah 14:12-14)

After his fall, what place did Satan visit?

He appeared in the Garden of Eden, where God had placed Adam and Eve. *You were in Eden, the garden of God."* (see Ezekiel 28:13).

After yielding to the voice of the serpent and disobeying God, how did Adam and Eve feel?

They were afraid and ashamed. (Review Genesis 3:7-10).

Where are Satan's headquarters today?

And the Lord said to Satan, "From where do you come?" So Satan answered the Lord and said, "From going to and fro on the earth, and from walking back and forth on it" (see Job 1:7).

Woe to the inhabitants of the earth and the sea! The devil has come down to you, having great wrath, because he knows that he has a short time (Revelation 12:12).

Chapter 2

BANISHED FROM EDEN

Through the fall, man forfeited all of his rights as a citizen of God's kingdom, and now must be dealt with as a rebel. He could no longer be trusted to live in the garden where the tree of life grew. If they ate from this fruit they would live in sin forever. Therefore, by the grace of God they were banished from Eden:

> *So He drove out the man; and He placed cherubim at the east of the garden of Eden, and a flaming sword which turned every way, to guard the way to the tree of life* (Genesis 3:24).

The fact that the tree of life remained in the garden, even though guarded by angels and a sword, was a ray of hope, signifying that since God did not uproot the tree one day its fruit may be eaten again.

God made man in His own image and likeness. He was a little lower than the angels (see Psalm 8:5). His destiny *was* to have dominion over the earth and to dwell there as an everlasting inheritance. *Then God blessed them, and God said to them, "Be fruitful and multiply; fill the earth, and subdue it; have dominion over the fish of the sea, over the birds of the air, and over every living thing that moves on the earth"* (Genesis 1:28). This eternal tenure was based upon one clear condition, the full and complete obedience to all of God's commands.

The issue was perfectly clear and understood. If man continued in obedience, he would have perpetual dominion. He would live forever! If he proved unfaithful and broke God's commands, he would forfeit his right to live. Man had a choice. The choice was his! That choice is now passed on to every person.

He lost it all

By their sin they lost all: their innocence, purity, happiness, and even their lives. Unfit to live in Eden, God drove them out and set mighty angels as guards to prevent their return. Mankind was now homeless and wonderers in a world that was shaken under the weight of God's judgment. Man's ties with his creator were severed. He had sold out to Satan, and had become his servant, *"Do you not know that to whom you present yourselves slaves to obey, you are that one's slaves whom you obey, whether of sin leading to death, or of obedience leading to righteousness?* (Romans 6:16). And *"Therefore, just as through one man sin entered the world, and death through sin, and thus death spread to all men, because all sinned"* (Romans 5:12). The propensity to sin entered humanity; and mankind became sinners **by nature.** Adam passed to all his descendants the inherent sinful nature that he possessed **because of his disobedience.** That nature is present from the moment of conception (see Psalm51:5) making it totally impossible for man to live in a way that pleases God. His descendents have added the guilt of their own transgressions. They may be prone to reproach Adam for his weakness, but they have done no better. They have all followed Adam's example, *"For all have sinned, and come short of the glory of God"* (Romans 3:23). What then? Are we better then they? Not at all! For we have previously charged both Jews and Greeks that they are all under sin. As it is written:

> *There is none righteous, no not one,*
> *There is none who understands;*
> *There is none who seeks after God.*
> *They have all turned aside;*
> *They have together become unprofitable*
> (Romans 3:9-12).

Humanity left stranded

Adam's fall left the entire human family stranded. Except for God's mercy there would have been absolutely no way of escape. In the parable of the rich man and Lazarus, Jesus likened sin to a great gulf which man is unable to cross (see Luke 16:26). *The sinner cannot save him/ herself.*

- His or her course spirals downward.
- His or her sinfulness increases with the years.
- His or her attempt to save them self only causes deeper sinking.

The history of humanity for 6000 years is one of increasing wickedness, and we are assured in the Bible that the last generation will be the worst. The apostle Paul declares: ***"But evil men and imposters will grow worse and worse, deceiving and being deceived"*** (2 Timothy 3:13).

Two Deaths

As a direct result of Adam's sin all men and women die the **natural death**. This is true of all humankind, as is testified to by the fact that all preceding generations have died. Today countless millions of men, women, and children are in the grave. At the same time millions are constantly passing on affecting each of us as we lose loved ones.

But these things terrible as they are do not reflect the primary result of sin. Beyond all of these is the **second death.** This second death will not be caused by so-called natural causes, but by the "lake of fire" which God Himself is preparing for the final destruction of the sin, sinners, and the devil along with his demons.

But thanks be to God there is a way of escape from the wages of sin (death). We hear Him speak in Isaiah 61:1-2,

"The Spirit of the Lord GOD is upon Me, because the
Lord, has anointed
Me
To preach good tidings to the poor;
He has sent Me to heal the brokenhearted,
To proclaim liberty to the captives,
And the opening of the prison to those who are bound;
To proclaim the acceptable year of the Lord,
And the day of vengeance of our
God;
To comfort all who mourn.

The "acceptable year of the Lord" (v. 2) is the same as "the day of salvation" (49:8) and "the year of My redeemed" (63:4). This is where Jesus stopped reading in the synagogue (Luke 4:19), indicating that the balance of the chapter (vv. 2b-11) waits for the second-coming of Christ, humankind's only Savior. He is the Authentic Christ!

STUDY SUMMARY

CHAPTER 2

BANISHED FROM EDEN

What was God's purpose for man?

"And God blessed them, saying, "Be fruitful, and multiply, and fill the waters in the seas, and let birds multiply on the earth" (Genesis 1:28).

"You have made him to have dominion over the works of Your hands; You have put all things under his feet, all sheep and oxen—even the beasts of the field, the birds of the air, and the fish of the sea that pass through the paths of the sea" (Psalm 8:6-8).

Man was to be in control of the earth as God's representative, but his appointment was conditioned upon *obedience* and *loyalty*. Should he sin, he would forfeit his *position* as ruler and even *life* itself.

What was the immediate result of Adam's sin?

"The Lord expelled Adam and Eve from His presence and the garden, their home. Adam was to till the ground from which he was taken. Their purity and innocence gone; they were now sinners.

How many were affected by Adam's sin?

*"Therefore, just as through one man sin entered the world, and earth through sin, and thus death spread to all men, because **all** sinned"* (Romans 5:12).

Having inherited Adam's sin, how does humankind add to their guilt?

All men and women have committed personal sin. *"For all have sinned and fall short of the glory of God"* (Romans 3:23).

> *As it is written: There is none righteous, no not one;*
> *There is none who understands;*
> *There is none who seeks after God.*
> *They have all turned aside;*
> *They have together become*
> *unprofitable;*
> *There is none who does good, no, not one*
> (Romans 3:10-12).

Chapter 3

THE INCARNATION OF CHRIST

Just before Adam and Eve were expelled from Eden, their Paradise home, they were given the wonderful promise that God, against whom they had rebelled, would send them a *Deliverer.* This Redeemer would bear the burden of man's transgression and would destroy Satan *[the spiritual serpent]* who had led them into sin.

This promise God had imbedded in the sharp rebuke uttered to the serpent, when He said: *"And I will put enmity between you and the woman, and between your seed and her Seed; He shall bruise your head, and you shall bruise His heel"* (Genesis 3:15).

I say again, this "first gospel" is prophetic of the struggle and its outcome between "your seed" (Satan and unbelievers who are called the devil's children in John 8:44) and "her Seed" (Christ, who is Eve's descendent and all those who are in Him).

After 4000 years

The time of waiting was long. For four thousand years the worshipers of God cherished *the promise*, waited, longed, and prayed for its fulfillment. I would imagine every godly mother in Israel had hoped that her son might be the promised Deliverer. One night in the little town of Bethlehem as the town was thronged with people who had traveled far and near for Caesar Augustus' census. For this census everyone had to appear in their hometown of birth. With no room in the inn this young couple from Nazareth ended up in the cattle stalls as many others no doubt did. With no fanfare a child was born to this young couple. While many lost hope, others like a group of godly shepherds still clung to the *promise* and *watched* for any possible sign of its fulfillment.

The Scripture says, *"And behold, and angel of the Lord stood before them, and the glory of the Lord shone around them, and they were greatly afraid. Then the angel said to them, "Do not be afraid, I bring you good tidings of great joy which shall be to all people. For there is born to you this day in the city of David a Savior, who is Christ the Lord. And this will be the sign to you: You will find a babe wrapped in swaddling clothes, lying in a manger."* And suddenly there was with the angel a multitude of the heavenly host praising God and saying:

> *"Glory" to God in the highest,*
> *And on earth peace, goodwill*
> *toward men!"*

This was the most beautiful message that had ever fallen on human ears. Their hopes had been realized. A Savior was born. Messiah had come. The *promise* that man would be able one day to regain all he had long ago lost in his Paradise was assured.

So it was, when the angels were gone from them into heaven that the shepherds said, to one another, "Let us now go to Bethlehem and see this thing that has come to pass, which the Lord has made known to us." And they came with haste and found Mary and Joseph, and the Babe lying in a manger. Now when they had seen *Him,* they made widely known the saying which was told them concerning the Child. And all those who heard it marveled at those things which were told them by the shepherds. But Mary kept all these things and pondered them in her heart. Then the shepherds returned, glorifying and praising God for all the things that they had heard and seen, as it was told them (Luke 2:15-20).

Who was this child?

Who was this child laid in a manger in Bethlehem? Why was His birth proclaimed by angelic visitors from heaven? How is He different from other people? These questions burned in the hearts of people then and these same questions [2000 years later] when answered individually by all humankind determine their eternal destiny.

At that time the Jews said, "He is only a man, and a very dangerous one at that. He ought to be put to death." Today millions who claim to praise and worship Him declare that He is the greatest and best man that ever lived; but they too deny that He was anything but human [Satan is making the most of this ignorance today, by trying to keep Jesus Christ out of the hearing of people]. Again, the questions, "Who do the crowds say that I am?" "Who do you say that I am?" (see Luke 9:18-20). There are millions of others, like Peter and the other disciples of old who declare Him to be the Christ, the very Son of the Living God and their Lord and Savior.

Seven hundred years before His birth, this child had been named. The inspired prophet Isaiah said: "Therefore the Lord Himself shall give you a sign; Behold, the virgin shall conceive and bear a son, and shall call His name Immanuel" (Isaiah 7:14). Matthew declares the birth of Jesus was the fulfillment of this prophecy, and the interpretation of His name was, *"God with us!"*

"So all this was done that it might be fulfilled which was spoken by the Lord through the prophet saying: *"Behold, the virgin shall be with child, and bear a Son, and they shall call His name Immanuel,"* which is translated, "God with us" (Matthew 1:22-23).

When speaking of His origin, Jesus Himself declared: *"I proceeded from the Father"* (John 8:42). Again, in His memorable prayer for His disciples, Jesus asserted His pre-existence as He entreated His Father: *"And now, O Father, glorify Me together with yourself, with the glory which I had with You before the world was"* (John 17:5). Earlier He had declared to the Pharisees concerning Himself: *"Before Abraham was, I AM"* (John 8:58).

Certainly the life of Christ did not begin in this lowly manger in Bethlehem. That was only an **incarnation.** He had existed from eternity. He had shared the companionship and the glory of God. Now He had *voluntarily* come into the world and taken upon

Himself the nature of fallen mankind [but without sin]. He had been born of a woman for the sole purposes:

- To destroy the works of the devil, his kingdom of darkness and all the works emerging from that realm of sin, sickness, disease, death and bondage are the works of the devil (see 1 John 3:5, 8).
- When Adam fell, God introduced substitutionary sacrifice for sin until Christ came to offer Himself as the perfect sacrifice. Every Old Testament sacrifice pointed to Christ's perfect *once-for-all* sacrifice. This was the supreme purpose of the incarnation. Only a perfect *sinless* man [Adam's state before his fall] could atone for sin. Christ fulfilled and abolished the animal sacrifices (see Leviticus 16:10-22; Isaiah 53:6; Hebrews 10:1-10; II Corinthians 5:21; Hebrews 2:9-14; 9:26; Mark 10:45; 1 John 3:5; John 1:29:36). Thus, providing a way for humankind out of the kingdom of darkness and into the kingdom of light with full reconciliation back to God by saving them from their sins.

Whether any individual will suffer the fate of hell or share the reward of the righteous in heaven is a matter of his or her own *choice*. God has placed the gift of eternal life within the reach of all who will accept it. It is a free gift. His invitation to His kingdom is to "whosoever will." (see Revelation 22:17). But man must choose.

"Let this mind be in you that was also in Christ Jesus, who being in the form of God, did not consider it robbery to be equal with God, but made Himself of no reputation, taking the form of a bondservant, and coming in the likeness of men. And being found in appearance as a man, He humbled Himself and became obedient to the *point of death,* even the death of the cross" (Philippians 2:5-8). The Apostle Paul also said concerning Christ: *"For by Him all things were created that are in heaven and that are on earth, visible, and invisible, whether thrones or dominions or principalities or powers. He is before all things, and in Him all things consist. And He is the Head of the body, the church, who is the beginning, the firstborn from the dead, that in all things He may have preeminence. For it pleased the Father that in Him all the fullness should dwell"* (Colossians 1:16-19).

"All things were made by Him declares the apostle John, and without Him was not anything made that was made" (John 1:3). On this important point the testimony of one other should suffice. Listen reverently. In Hebrews 1:8-10, the Witness now is none other than the Mighty God Himself:

But to the Son He says:

"Your throne, O God, is forever and ever;
A scepter of righteousness is the scepter of Your
kingdom.
You have loved righteousness and hated lawlessness;
Therefore God, Your God, has anointed You
With the oil of gladness more than
Your companions"
And:
You, Lord, in the beginning laid the foundation of the
earth,
And the heavens and the work of
Your hands.

STUDY SUMMARY

CHAPTER 3

THE INCARNATION OF CHRIST

Where was Jesus born?

He was born in Bethlehem of Judea, A little village about three miles from Jerusalem. (see Matthew 2:1).

To whom did the angels appear at this time?

To shepherds in a field keeping watch over their flocks (see Luke 2:8-9).

What startling announcement did the angel make to these shepherds?

Then the angel of the Lord said to them, "Do not be afraid, for behold, I bring you good tidings of great joy which will be to all people. For there is born to you this day in the city of David a Savior, who is Christ the Lord. And this will be a sign to you: You will find a babe wrapped in swaddling clothes, lying in a manger." (Luke 2:10-12).

In the announcement to the shepherds, who did the angel say the newborn child was?

"A Savior, which is Christ the Lord" (Luke 2:11).

Did Christ exist before He was born in Bethlehem?

"And now, O Father, glorify Me together with Yourself, with the glory which I had with You before the world was" (John 17:5).

What was the purpose of His incarnation?

He was manifested to take away our sins and in Him is no sin (1 John 3:5). *For this purpose the Son of God was manifested, that He might destroy the works of the devil* (v. 8).

SECTION II

The Authentic Christ

Chapter 4

JESUS CHRIST: THE SON OF GOD

If so many claim Jesus Christ was only a man; then likewise Christianity to them is just another religion of idolatry, and His death on Calvary was entirely meaningless to the rest of humanity. However, He is divine, the very Son of God, omniscient, and omnipotent, the Scriptures everywhere declare. Once we seek the truth, we find ourselves face to face with the enormous truth that Jesus Christ of Nazareth was none other than "God manifest in the flesh!" The Son of God became incarnate and came down to dwell with the human family. In his announcement of the birth of Jesus, the prophet Isaiah declared, *"Behold, the virgin shall conceive and bear a Son, and shall call His name Immanuel, which being interpreted is, God with us"* (Matthew 1:23; Isaiah 7:14).

The question of Jesus' deity must be satisfactorily answered before we can conceive of His mission here and His death on Calvary. On many occasions Jesus, Himself proclaimed His deity. He declares, *"I came forth from the Father and have come into the world"* (John 16:28). *If I do not do the works of My Father, do not believe Me, believe the works, that you may know and believe that the Father is in Me and I in Him"* (John 10:37, 38).

Thus, Jesus leaves no question as to His origin. He knew that it was all-important that the church should fully understand His Godhead. This must be the foundation of our faith in Him, if Jesus Christ is to be authentic. To reject His deity is to render Him a mere man and His offer of salvation to sinners merely a joke. Jesus is the self-existent One, who is from everlasting to everlasting.

Eternal Love

If Jesus is eternal, then His love is eternal also! He is the same yesterday, today and forever, the unchangeable God. One fault His enemies found with Jesus, He was a friend of sinners. Jesus hates sin, but its presence in the hearts of humans does not diminish His love for *them*. **It was for sinners that He died!**

"For when we were still without strength, in due time Christ died for the ungodly. For scarcely for a righteous man will one die, But God demonstrates His own love toward us, in that while we were still sinners, Christ died for us" (Romans 5:6-8). Jesus sees in the sinner, not what he is today, but what he or she may become through His grace and love. Constantly He pleads for sinners to *turn to Him and be saved.*

A couple of years ago when it became apparent that the great Evangelist Billy Graham would no longer personally lead the great crusades; a number of men stepped forth with the confession that they were to be his replacement. I believe that it's time for the church to stand up corporately in unity and like Jesus, love sinners just as they are. However, like Jesus we to must love them too much to leave them as they are! Jesus gives all saints a charge, *"You did not choose Me, but I chose you and appointed you that you should go and bear fruit, and that your fruit should remain, that whatever you ask the Father in My name he may give you. These things I command you, that you love one another."* The Apostle Paul assures us, *"Being confident of this very thing that He who has begun a good work in you will complete it until the day of Jesus Christ"* (Philippians 1:6). Paul was convinced that the "you" in this passage pertained to the Philippian church [today it fits the church at large in America] not isolated individuals. There is no room for argument or doubt. Jesus Christ, who was preached to the Gentiles, believed on in the world, and who ascended to heaven in the sight of his disciples was God manifested in the flesh. Truly, He was the Lord of glory. Simply put the church must obey His commission to "go into all the world" and all of the church must go!

Jesus Christ is able to save

What conclusion can we make from this tremendous amount of scriptural evidence? The fact of the matter is this: Jesus of Nazareth, who lived among humankind and died on a Roman cross, was the Son of God. His claim was true, when He declared, "All power is given unto Me in heaven and in the earth." Equipped with this power, He undertook the redemption of man, and was able therefore, to offer the indescribable *gift of eternal life* to all who would accept Him as *their* Savior. The advent of Christ among humanity was the most transcendent display of divine love, wisdom, and goodness ever known in the universe. Those who deny His deity and His vicarious sacrifice for their sins do so only at their own risk and those who die in their rejection are doomed to eternal destruction, which is the possible destination of all who *rebel* against God.

What kind of person can pass by this glorious *truth* with indifference? Yet, some of the worst undermining of Jesus comes from sources you would least expect: biblical scholars. How can this possibly happen? The answer is as old as Adam and Eve, it is the tendency of fallen humans to trust their own *minds* over the *truth* of God's revelation. Jesus made humble submission to God's authority the prerequisite for knowing and understanding His words: *"If anyone wills to do His will, he shall know concerning the doctrine, whether I speak on My own authority"* (John 7:17). Those who are committed to doing God's will are guided by Him in the affirmation of His *truth.* God's truth is self-authenticating through the teaching ministry of the Holy Spirit (see John 16:13; 1 John 2:20, 27).

Miracles authenticate His Deity

The omnipotence of Christ is clearly revealed in His miracles. To the leper He said, "I will "be thou clean;" to the blind man, "Receive thy sight;" to the raging sea, "Peace be still;" and, miracle of grace, He said to the sinner, "Your sins be forgiven you." All these were accomplished by the power of His Word. Isaiah asks,

Have you not known?
Have you not heard?
The everlasting God, the Lord,
The Creator of the ends of the earth,
Neither faints nor is weary.
His understanding is unsearchable,
And to those who have no might He
increases strength;
even the youths shall faint and be weary,
And the young men shall utterly fall,
But those who wait on the Lord
Shall renew their strength;
They shall mount up with wings like eagles,
They shall run and not be weary,
They shall walk and not faint
(Isaiah 40:28-31).

Come, then, let us wait on Him that we may renew our strength. He is omnipotent to deliver, all-powerful to conquer all the fiery passions of the flesh, and to give victory over every temptation. Think about it, He can calm all fears, defeat all foes, dispel all darkness and make the life to become one glorious dawn. But all of this He can do only if we let Him! He says, *"Behold I stand at the door and knock. If anyone hears My voice and opens the door, I will come in to him and dine with him, and he with Me"* (Revelation 3:20). He will not coerce nor force His way in. "But as many as receive Him, to them He gives power to become the sons of God"(see John 1:12).

He knows all things

Only God has the divine attribute of omniscience. A mere human, though he or she may be the best of teachers, cannot know the heart. Since we cannot know our own hearts because they are very deceitful, we should praise God and rejoice, because there is One who can search them and discover what is there. Certainly we should pray with David, *"Search me, O God, and know my heart; try me, and know my anxieties; and see if there is any wicked way in me, and lead me in the way everlasting"* (Psalm 139:23, 24). The loving invitation of Jesus to each one is, *"My son, [daughter] give Me your heart."* He desires to search it now, so that in the final day sin will not be found there. We must lay our hearts bare before Him. Corruption and sin we would never admit existing in our heart—we can tell Him all about it! He bids us, "Cast all your cares upon Him; for He cares for you" (see 1 Peter 5:7).

He offers to cleanse the soul that is open to Him. Then and only then will we be able to sing with David: *"I acknowledged my sin to you, and my iniquity I have not hidden, I said, "I will confess my transgressions to the Lord, and You forgave the iniquity of my sin"* (Psalm 32:5).

STUDY SUMMARY

CHAPTER 4

JESUS: THE SON OF GOD

What did Jesus say concerning His origin?

"I came forth from the Father and have come into the world. Again, I leave the world and go to the Father" (John 16:28).

What did Christ claim to have?

He claimed to have inherent immortality. "For as the Father has life in Himself. So He has granted the Son to have life in Himself" (John 5:26). "In Him was life; and the life was the light of men" (John 1:4).

Besides Jesus is there any other Savior?

"Neither is there salvation in any other; for there is no other name under heaven given among men, whereby we must be saved" (Acts 4:12).

Who did the Apostle Paul say Jesus was?

He declared the deity of Jesus by saying, "God was manifested in the flesh, justified in the Spirit, seen by angels, preached among the Gentiles, believed on in the world, received up in glory" (1 Timothy 3:16). Jesus was God the Son.

Who can search a heart and tell what is there?

God can! David prayed, "Search me O God, and know my heart: try me, and know my anxieties, and see if there is any wicked way in me, and lead me in the way everlasting" (Psalm 139:23, 24).

Chapter 5

JESUS CHRIST: THE MAN

Jesus Christ was not only divine, He was also human. He was born of woman, came under the law, and took upon Himself our very nature.

He had to become Man

In His deity only, Christ could not fully atone for the sins of humanity. The sacrifice must also have the human element in it. Therefore, in dying for our sins, Christ had to die as a man. Prior to His death, He suffered in man's flesh.

"For indeed He does not give aid to angels, but He does give aid to the seed of Abraham. Therefore, in all things He had to be made like His brethren, that He might be a merciful and faithful High Priest in things pertaining to God, to make propitiation for the sins of the people. "For in that He Himself has suffered, being tempted, He is able to aid those who are tempted" (Hebrews 2:16-18).

His death and burial in the tomb also had to be in the flesh, so that there would be assurance of a resurrection from the dead for all those who should believe on Him. The Apostle Paul admonishes: *"For if the dead do not rise, then Christ is not risen. And if Christ is not risen, your faith is futile; you are still in your sins! Then also those who have fallen asleep in Christ have perished. If in this life only we have hope in Christ, we are of all men the most pitiable"* (1 Corinthians 15:16-23).

Christ's virgin birth is so beautifully set in the angel Gabriel's announcement to Mary. "Now in the sixth month the angel Gabriel was sent by God to a city of Galilee named Nazareth, to a virgin betrothed to a man whose name was Joseph, of the house of David. The virgin's name was Mary. And having come in, the angel said to her, *"Rejoice, highly favored one, the Lord is with you; blessed are you among women!"*

But when she saw him, she was troubled at his saying, and considered what manner of greeting this was. Then the angel said to her, *"Do not be afraid, Mary for you have found favor with God. And behold, you will conceive in your womb and bring forth a Son, and shall call His name Jesus. He will be great, and will be called the Son of the Highest; and the Lord God will give Him the throne of His father, David. And He will reign over the house of Jacob forever, and of His kingdom there will be no end."* Then Mary said to the angel, "How can this be, since I do not know a man?" And the angel answered and said to her, *"The Holy Spirit will come upon you, and the power of the Highest will overshadow you; therefore, also, that Holy One who is to be born will be called the Son of God"* (Luke 1:26-35).

It was of human flesh and blood that Jesus partook. He became a member of the human race. He became like men. The Scripture says, "Inasmuch then as the children have partaken of flesh and blood, He Himself likewise shared in the same, that through death He might destroy him who had the power of death, that is, the devil, and release those who through fear of death were all their lifetime subject to bondage. For indeed He does not give aid to angels, but He does give aid to the seed of Abraham. Therefore, in all things He had to be made like His brethren, that He might be a merciful and faithful High Priest in things pertaining to God, to make propitiation for the sins of the people. For, in that He Himself has suffered being tempted, He is able to aid those who are tempted" (Hebrews 2:14-18). Here then was real humanity. It was not the nature of angels that He assumed, but that of Abraham. He was *"in all things made like unto His brethren."*

- He became one of them.
- He was subject to temptation.
- He knew the pain of suffering.
- He was not a stranger to the common problems of humankind.

For we do not have a High Priest who cannot sympathize with our weaknesses, but was in all points tempted as we are, yet without sin. (Hebrews 4:15).

- In order to understand the weakness of human nature, He had to experience it.
- In order for Him to be sympathetic with men in their trials, He also had to be tried.
- He must experience hunger, weariness, disappointment, sorrow, and persecution.
- He must tread the same paths, live under the same circumstances, and die the same death.

Therefore, He became bone of our bone and flesh of our flesh. His incarnation was in actual humanity. In fact, His union was so complete of the divine and human, that when the Lord arose from the grave and ascended again to sit at the right hand of God, He went as a man there to represent the human race as our older Brother and Advocate.

God's eternal Gift

God's gift of His Son to the human race was, therefore a complete gift. The Father didn't loan His Son to the human race. He was an outright gift. He sits at the right hand of the Father today *clothed in human flesh.* He still bears the marks of the Crucifixion in His hands, feet, and side. Though now glorified and exalted above all, He is still Christ Jesus "The Man" and will remain so throughout eternity. Give me Jesus!

He Humbled Himself

Christ's humiliation later led to His great exaltation. He is the ultimate example. Let this mind be in you which was also in Christ Jesus, who being in the form of God, did not consider it robbery to be equal with God, but made Himself of no reputation, taking the form of a bondservant, and coming in the likeness of men. And being found in appearance as a man, He humbled Himself and became obedient to the point of death, even the death of the cross.

Therefore, God also has highly exalted Him and gave Him the name which is above every name, that at the name of Jesus every knee should bow, of those in heaven, and of those on earth, and of those under the earth, and that every tongue should confess that Jesus Christ is Lord, to the glory of God the Father. (Philippians 2:5-11).

The Union of the Divine and Human

This incarnation of God is the mystery of the ages. That God should tabernacle in human flesh is no doubt the most staggering **truth** of all times. There was absolutely no other way for the great chasm to be **bridged.** Thus, the union of the divine and human natures was so that Christ could fulfill in His *One Person,* that which was separate and distinct in the Old Testament mediatory ministry. Additionally, the High Priest and the sacrifice were separate. In Christ as the God-Man both are brought together in one. He was truly God and truly man. In no other way could the Son of God qualify as the Redeemer of humankind:

- It had to be made by One who could properly represent both side, God's side and humanity's side.
- This could only be done by a God-man.
- There must be a union of the two *natures.*
- God must come down to humanity in order to lift humans up to Himself.

The first Adam had but one nature, human nature, and it had the liability to sin and did sin. Animal sacrifices were substituted because of their sinless nature; however, they could not atone for human nature, the lesser could not atone for the greater, God had to bring in a perfect human nature to atone for sinful human nature. The last Adam, the Second Man, was the Lord from heaven and as the first of the *new creation* had two natures, divine and human. His human nature was sinless [I repeat] as Adam's was before the fall. Because it was to divine nature which assumed the human nature there was no liability to fall, no response to sin. Jesus was an incarnation. ***"God was in Christ reconciling the world unto Himself" (II Corinthians 5:18-21).*** Adam was a creation, but he was not God incarnate. Thus Jesus, as Mediator and Priest (Divine) was able to offer Himself, His own sinless body and blood as the sacrifice and offering (human) and made possible reconciliation between God and man. Give Him praise and glory!

It was therefore, Jesus Christ the God-man who suffered and died on the cross for sin. It was the Savior who was both divine and human who offered Himself up in man's behalf. This was the *basis* of the adequacy of His atoning sacrifice. In Jacob's dream at Bethel he saw a ladder reaching from earth to heaven Angels were descending and ascending on it. Jesus later declared Himself to be this ladder *connecting* earth and heaven, and that through **Him alone** humankind could find their way from this sin-cursed earth back to God.

- By His *human nature* as the Son of Man, Jesus can reach down to the very lowest depth of human sorrow and suffering and get a hold of the worst sinners.
- By His *divine nature* as the Son of God, Jesus is able to lift these suffering and down-trodden men and women up to God in heaven.
- By His *human nature,* He can sympathize with struggling sinners.
- By His *divine nature,* He can save them from their sins and finish them for immortality and for heaven. Give Him praise!

Look! The Son of God presenting Himself before the Father and offering to come into the world to save lost humankind! And look at the great heart of the Father so moved by His love for sinners the He freely *"gave His only begotten Son, that whosoever believeth in Him should not perish, but have eternal life"* (John 3:16 KJV). "Seeing then that we have a great High Priest who has passed through the heavens, Jesus the Son of God, let us hold fast *our* confession. For we do not have a High Priest who cannot sympathize with our weaknesses, but was in all points tempted as *we are, yet* without sin. Let us therefore come boldly to the throne of grace that we may obtain mercy and find grace to help in time of need (Hebrews 4:14-16). **It was at the throne of God that Christ made atonement for sins, and it is there that grace is dispensed to believers for <u>all issues of life!</u> The Holy Spirit calls for all to come confidently before God's throne to receive mercy and grace through Jesus Christ (see Hebrews 7:25; 10:22; Matthew 27:51).**

STUDY SUMMARY

CHAPTER 5

JESUS CHRIST: THE MAN

Who did Jesus declare Himself to be?

"When Jesus came into the region of Caesarea Philippi, He asked His disciples, saying, "Who do men say that, *I the Son of Man am?" (Matthew 4:14-16).*

NOTE: Jesus had a dual nature. He was not only "the Son of God" but also "the Son of man." He was born of woman, but His conception was brought about through the operation of the Holy Spirit. He had no human father (See Matthew 16:13).

Why was it necessary for the Son of God to become a man in order to become our Savior?

"That He might become a merciful and faithful High Priest" (Hebrews 2:17). Also He had to be tempted and tried as men are, in order that He could sympathize with them in their suffering.

After His resurrection, was Christ still in human form?

Yes, He appeared to His frightened disciples and said to them, *"Behold My hands and My feet, that it is I Myself. Handle Me and see, for a spirit does not have flesh and bones as you see I have. When He had said this, He showed them His hands and His feet. But while they still did not believe for joy, and marveled, He said to them, "Have you any food here?" So they gave Him a piece of a broiled fish and some honeycomb. And He took it and ate in their presence"* (Luke 24:36-43).

Did Jesus go back to heaven as a man?

Yes. He was talking to His disciples on the Mount of Olives, and the Scripture says, *"So then, after the Lord had spoken to them, He was received up into heaven, and sat down at the right hand of God"* (Mark 16:19).

What is Christ said to be?

"There is one God and one Mediator between God and men, the Man Jesus Christ" (see 1 Timothy 2:5).

Chapter 6

HIS BLOOD FOR OUR SINS

The atonement that Jesus Christ made for sinners by His death on the cross is the central fact of the gospel. It is the sun around which all other *truths* revolve. In reality, it is the very *essence* of the gospel; if it is taken away, nothing of the gospel remains. It forms the foundation of *the* faith, the very basis of the sinner's hope.

Over the years much has been done based on the evolutionary theory, which seeks to block the stream of Christ's precious blood; which was shed for sinful humanity. All of this is aimed at robbing Christ of His divinity and power. If the fountain could be stopped, the doom of the whole world would be sealed; and no human being would ever be reconciled back to God. For, *"without shedding of blood there is no remission" (Hebrew 9:22).*

It would be impossible to study all of the evidence of Christ's deity and greatness without coming to the conclusion that the atonement of Christ has infinite value. If Christ had been a mere man or even an angel, His death would have no meaning to a lost world for the substitution death of a man or angel:

- Could *never* satisfy divine justice,
- Could *never* honor a divine law.
- Could *never* accomplish the salvation of the soul; and humans would still be in their sins.

Law demands Death

As I pointed out earlier, Adam and all generations following him have broken God's moral law and the law demanded *death* to transgressors. Satan has a great move on among some denominations to set aside the necessity of Christ's death. A reign of demonic terror over the entire world was set lose by the attempts of mankind to suppress the name of Jesus. Christ Jesus is God's *only* guarantee of reconciliation.

There is only one way to save doomed humankind from eternal death, and that was for God, as man, to become humanity's surety, assume their guilt and die in their stead. This He did not hesitate to do!

God gave His only-begotten Son as a ransom for the fallen race. When Satan took Jesus to the mountaintop and offered to give Him the kingdoms of the world with their earthly glory, he was offering Him the crown *without the cross.* It was to be a *shortcut* to securing the rule of the world. Imagine if you will, a kingdom made up of sinners. They would have become Jesus' subjects. However, from the beginning God declared that He would *rule* only over those who were righteous. Although Christ is a friend of sinners and desires to bring about their salvation; He is not their God and Father! Jesus declared to those who rejected Him, *"You are of your father, the devil, and the desires of your father you want to do"* (John 8:44). In order for the earth to be restored to His kingdom, and for men and women to become His subjects, He had to first prepare the way for sinners to be transformed into saints. He could accomplish this only by going to the cross; if sinners were to be freed from their sentence of death. He must die for them, for "without shedding of *blood* there is no remission." (Hebrews 9:22). Their blood or His it was their decision then; and it's our decision today! **There is no other way!** The authentic Christ endured the cross, thus winning *the right* to save humans from sin and its penalty, and *finally* bring reconciliation with God.

With His Stripes we are healed

Christ presented Himself a *sacrifice* for our sins. His sacrifice was so complete, that His subsequent priestly ministry was so effective that through these means the sins of His people may be *entirely blotted out.* Listen to the prophet, *"But He was wounded for our transgressions, He was bruised for our iniquities; the chastisement for our peace was upon Him. And by His stripes we are healed. All we like sheep have gone astray; we have turned, every one, to his own way; and the LORD has laid on Him the iniquity of us all"* (Isaiah 53:5-6).

On the cross, in His own body Jesus bore every weakness and burden that could come on a fallen sinful race. First Peter 2:24 says, "[He] Himself who took our sins in His own body on the tree, that we, having died to sins, might live for righteousness by whose stripes you were healed." Jesus did not bear only our *sins* on the cross, but also our *sicknesses.* Physical healing is a part of redemption. You have the legal right to perfect health because every sickness, every infirmity, every pain that sin brought upon the human race was laid upon the body of Jesus as He hung on the cross. He was the sinner's substitute. Everything that was due to the sinner was laid on Him!

Having heard the revelation of truth concerning your healing it is up to you to accept this truth by faith. Sometimes I think we forget in our counsel to insure that the counselee understands that faith comes by hearing. You must decide that Jesus is your Healer [Doctor], No one else can make that decision for you. If your answer is yes; then you must commit to that decision without wavering. Derek Prince used Billy Graham as an example in one of his books to express this very point. He states, "Basically, what Billy Graham did for about forty-five minutes was preach what the Scriptures teach about forgiveness of sin and salvation. Then having preached, he invited the people to *make a decision.* He always called them out and demanded that they make a personal commitment. The point Dr. Prince made here is that the same truth applies to physical healing. You hear the Word and then make a decision. God said, *"I am the LORD who heals you"* (see Exodus 15:26). This testifies to the mercy and power of God![3]

It is still true: all healing comes from God.

His blood brought *redemption* to *us.* Pilate declared: *"I find no cause of death in Him."* O, How true! The cause of death was in us. We had to pay the wages of sin; we were under condemnation, and Jesus stepped in and took our place and punishment. I urge that each of us contend for the faith. The faith is the truth of God's Word. Stand on it! What a spectacle, the Son of God pouring out His life's blood for us, who were sinners that He might purchase the right to transfer His righteousness and purity to us. Certainly we should remember that all of the above is dependent upon our being in right relationship with Christ and one another. Hearing and receiving the Word is key to physical healing. It is the Word that sets us free.

Only *the blood of Jesus Christ* can cleanse us from all sin, making it possible for imperfect believers to have fellowship with a holy God.

Hearing the Spirit

In the prior section we saw how it is necessary that a person who hears the Word of God and takes action by faith receives physical healing. Along that same line, the Apostle John admonishes the churches to "hear what the Spirit is saying to the churches" (see

Revelation 2:7). Hearing the Spirit and acting by faith will result in our spiritual healing individually and corporately.

I read an article some time ago concerning how difficult the task was for NASA to keep the spacecraft on course, corrections were made periodically because of space wobble or other interferences. Jesus established His church, The Holy Spirit came and through the Apostle Peter, the fisher of men made the catch; then the Apostle Paul, the tentmaker, formed them as he planted churches throughout.

I believe today the Spirit is working through the Apostle John, the repairer of the nets, to restore and bring the church [the Body of Christ] to its full potential prior to the Lord's return for her. Though these great men of God have been gone for centuries their work remains through the Word of God. Today the Church is going through a restoration process by which the "spots and wrinkles" [wrong minds and perceptions] are being taken out [through the truth of God's Word] and made overcomers [through the Spirit]. The overcomer is the believer who perseveres in obedience of our Lord's commands and victoriously overcomes in the face of trials. Notice the profile of the overcomer according Revelation 2-3:

- The overcomer in [the church at Ephesus] rejects evil, perseveres, and has patience; the Lord promises that he or she will eat from the tree of life (see Revelation 2:7).
- The overcomer in [the church at Smyrna] gracefully bears suffering; the Lord promises a crown of life (v.11).
- The overcomer in [the church at Pergamos] keeps the faith of Christ; the Lord promises hidden manna and a stone with a new name on it (v.17).
- The overcomer in [the church at Thyatira] keeps the Lord's works [love, service, patience greater than the first] until the end; the Lord promises the overcomer will rule over nations and receive morning star. (v.26).
- The overcomer in [the church at Sardis] has kept the faith; the Lord promises the faithful will be honored and dressed in white. (3:5).

- The overcomer in [the church at Philadelphia] perseveres in the faith, keeps the word of Christ, and honors His name; the Lord promises a place in God's presence, a new name, and a New Jerusalem. (v.12).
- The overcomer in [the church of the *people* at Laodicia] is to be zealous and repent then; the Lord promises they will share His throne. (v. 21).

It is important to note as you read the verses of Scripture above, the character qualities of the overcomer references the believers in the church during the various periods of church history. The church of the last period [Laodicia] does not receive a commendation from the Lord; however, those who do repent and are zealous will share the throne with Christ. Isn't grace amazing? I believe the church of the Ladiceans depict the last days church. Therefore, the Christian must always be ready for Jesus' coming. Christ promised that His return would be sudden, that expected suddenness is an incentive to persevere in faithful service to Him.

As you read through the writings of the Apostle John you can feel his fatherly love as he urges all believers to make sure they are in right relationship with God and one another; thereby gaining immunity from the great deception that Satan is pulling off theologically in the churches today. John constantly urges the believer to love God and one another. Jesus emphasized the importance of love, as it is the one characteristic that separates the authentic Christian from the rest and even the world can identify them.

Much of the popular theology today is focused on the self. For example many ask how can I escape the great financial collapse which even the world knows is coming? Many are preaching that heaping up material goods such as gold and silver is the answer. The Bible admonishes all humanity to focus on God's solution, the authentic Christ, who promises to keep the believers from the hour of trial [indicating that He will remove them before this period of unparalleled trouble]. Three views shape the theology concerning the disposition of the believer:

- The first is that believers are overcomers and failure to overcome means there was no true salvation experience for that individual.
- The second holds that the promises are experienced only for believers who are faithful and obedient and failure to overcome means there has been a loss of salvation.
- The third is that the promises are experienced only by believers who are faithful and obedient and failure to overcome means a loss of rewards, not salvation. While we may encounter difficulties with all three of them, the third is most consistent with the characteristics of the overcomer passages that we observed above. In 1 Corinthians 3:13-15, we are told, *"Each one's work will become clear; for the day will declare it, because it will be revealed by fire, and the fire will test each one's work, of what sort it is. If anyone's work which he has built on endures, he will receive a reward. If anyone's work is burned, he will suffer loss; but he himself will be saved, yet so as through fire."*

God used Paul to lay the foundation at Corinth, and the foundation was Jesus Christ as preached in the Gospel. Others such as Apollos came along and built on that foundation and others after him. Paul warns that, "Each one should be take heed how [he or she] builds." (v.10). He then describes three kinds of Christian builders. Warren Wiersbe wrote of these three workers:

1. The wise builder (v. 14).

The first worker uses lasting materials (gold, silver, jewels) and not the cheap, shabby things of the world (wood, hay, stubbles). This builder seeks to honor Christ, aiming for quality that will glorify Christ, not quantity that will win the praise of men. Wise builders use the Word, prayer, and they are dependent upon the Spirit of God; as a result their work is lasting. When the fires try their work in glory, it will stand!

2. The worldly builder (v. 15).

The second builder uses materials that cannot stand the test. This is the Christian worker who is in a hurry to build a crowd, but does not take time to build a church. The materials come from the world, wood, hay, stubble. These people do not *test people's professions* by the Word to see if they are truly born again; they merely take them into the church rejoicing in the statistics. When this ministry is tested by fire, it burns up. The worker will be saved, but there is no reward. Like Lot, the worker will be saved as by fire.

3. The Destroyer (v. 17).

The destroyer does not build the church but tears it down. The word "defile" in v. 17 means "destroy." There are selfish Christian workers who destroy local churches instead of building them up. God has a severe judgment awaiting them. The Spirit used Paul to warn the church at Corinth, likewise He is using the Apostle John to warn the churches today. The Lord Jesus is seeking entrance into His own church today. He is the authentic Christ seeking *renewed fellowship*. The church's proper response is to *repent* and move away from a lukewarm spiritual state. Like the Laodiceans, many churches are spiritually blind to the truth and need to change their perspective and seek the spiritual riches of Jesus, the ultimate Overcomer.[4] In 1 John 1:6-7, the Scripture warns:

"If we say that we have fellowship with Him, and
walk in darkness, we lie and do not practice the truth.
But if we walk in the light as He is in the light,
we have fellowship with one another,
and the blood of Jesus His Son
cleanses us from all sin.

STUDY SUMMARY

CHAPTER 6

HIS BLOOD FOR OUR SINS

What does the Bible say will take away sin?

"The blood of Jesus Christ His Son cleanses us from all sin. (see 1 John 1:7).

Was it necessary for Christ to die in His behalf?

No. (see Luke 23:22).

For what reason then, did He die?

"But we see Jesus, who was made a little lower than the angels for the suffering of death, crowned with glory and honor, that He by the grace of God should taste death for every man" (Hebrews 2:9).

What sentence had been pronounced upon the human family?

"Wherefore, as by one man sin entered into the world, and death by sin; and so death passed upon all men, for that all have sinned" (Romans 5:12).

What did Christ's death accomplish for us?

"In whom we have redemption through His blood, the forgiveness of sins, according to the riches of His grace" (Ephesians 1:7).

Are any too sinful to come to God?

"This is a faithful saying, and worthy of all acceptances, that Christ Jesus came into the world to save sinners; of whom I am chief" (1 Timothy 1:15).

SECTION III

Salvation in No Other

Chapter 7

WHAT MUST I DO TO BE SAVED?

The greatest question of which all human beings are confronted [individually] is: "What must I do to be saved?" This question comes to every individual for "all have sinned and fall short of the glory of God" (see Romans 3:23). Human beings by nature are lost! No man or woman has the slightest claim upon immortality. Immortality has been the quest of man for six thousand years. In the 4th grade, I remember studying in Geography, how Ponce de Leon stepped upon the shores of Florida, he announced that he had discovered the fountain of perpetual youth; but those who drank quickly found it to be a disillusion.

The Illusion

I believe individuals of every generation and in every nation have sought eternal life. Who has not said with the rich young ruler who came to Jesus one day and asked, "What must I do to inherit eternal life?" Hundreds of religions have emerged prescribing this or that method of reaching the goal; yet in the minds of millions the question has not found a satisfactory answer.

When the Philippian jailer, who along with his family was converted under the preaching of the great Apostle Paul, pressed for an answer to the great question, Paul replied without the slightest hesitation, "Believe on the Lord Jesus Christ, and you will be saved, and your household" (Acts16:31). Later as He wrote to the believers in Rome, he declared, *"But what does it say? The Word is near you, in your mouth and in your heart"(that is the word of faith which we preach): that if you confess with your mouth the Lord Jesus and believe in your heart that God has raised Him from the dead, you will be saved. For with the heart one believes unto righteousness, and with the mouth confession is made unto salvation.*" For the Scripture says, "*Whoever believes on Him will not be put to shame*" (Romans 10:8-10).

Man cannot save Himself

Prayerfully it should be seen as a fundamental fact, man cannot save himself. No number of good deeds, self-abasement, philanthropy can remove the guilt of sin from the human soul. If any individual at all is saved he or she must have a Savior; and the only Savior of man is Jesus Christ. Do you know Him?

Religion after religion requires that the individual must clean them self up to be acceptable. Christianity is the very antithesis of that. It is impossible for anyone to lift himself or herself by their own strength from the mire and filth of sin, but each individual is offered cleansing, pardon, and salvation through the power and intervention of another. Jesus does not hold the sinner off until he has first cleansed his own heart (an accomplishment that would be altogether impossible), but He boldly extends the universal invitation:

> *Look to Me, and be saved,*
> *All you ends of the earth!*
> *For I am God, and there is no other*
> (Isaiah 45:22).

The vilest sinner may come and find deliverance from his sins: but no man or woman, regardless of how righteous they may appear in their own eyes, can save them self from sin's guilt and power. Neither is there a legitimate excuse for their sins. If the deliverance offered by Christ is not accepted by the sinner, he or she is utterly lost and absolutely without hope!

Not of works

During the Easter celebrations it is not uncommon to find people in many parts of the world who desiring salvation will seek it through some method of self-inflicted penance, or punishment supposing that in this way they may find God's favor [some are actually crucified or beaten with 39 stripes]. But that is not the way of salvation:

For by grace you have been saved through faith, and that not of yourselves; it is the gift of God, not of works that any man shall boast" (Ephesians 2:8-9).

Even *service* for Christ and humanity, as good as it may be, will not bring salvation. No one through their deeds of kindness and mercy can bribe God to grant the gift of eternal life. Though a man may bestow all his goods to feed the poor and give his body to be burned, it would profit him nothing so far as obtaining salvation is concerned.

- Service for others is not a means of salvation; but it is the *fruit* of salvation.
- It is not service but *faith* that brings salvation.
- People are not saved by anything they may do for God; but by what *He* does for them.
- Jesus *saves*, and apart from Him there is no salvation.

Jesus said, "I am the door, if any man [woman] enter in he [she] shall be saved." But He added, "He that enters not by the door . . . . but climbs up by some other way, is a thief and a robber"(John 10:1,9). It is such a pity that today untold millions have been deceived and are *striving to climb up some other way* rather than seeking salvation through simple faith in the Lord Jesus Christ. Years ago when I was stationed at Fort Bliss, Texas one of my tasks was to deliver fuel to various missile sites in the desert. It was not uncommon to see a beautiful welcoming lake stretched out before me in the heat of the day. The only problem was I was never able to reach the lake because it ran away from me. It was not a lake at all. It was a mirage of the desert. It was a delusion. As I sit here pondering our journey to an endless eternity that picture of the mirage in the desert is exactly the picture of human life without God.

- Without God life is defeated.
- Without God life's true aim is missed and lost.
- Without God men and women stumble on aimlessly following the mirage [illusion of life]; as it runs away before them.
- Listen to what the Bible has to say about this condition, *"Having no hope and without God in the world." (Ephesians 2:12).* Like the Gentiles in this passage of Scripture, today people have so many gods; they don't recognize the true God because they do not want Him. According to Romans 1:18-25, humankind is conscious of God's existence, power, and divinity through general revelation.

Notice, *"For the wrath of God is revealed from heaven against all ungodliness and unrighteousness of men, who suppress the truth in unrighteousness, because what may be known of God is manifest in them, for God has shown it to them. For since the creation of the world His invisible attributes are clearly seen, being understood by the things that are made, even His eternal power and Godhead, so that they are without excuse, because, although they knew God, they did not glorify Him as God, nor were thankful, but became futile in their thoughts, and their foolish hearts darkened. Professing to be wise, they became fools, and changed the glory* *of the incorruptible God into an image made like corruptible man and birds and four-footed animals and creeping things. Therefore **God also gave them up** to uncleanness, in the lusts of their hearts, to dishonor their bodies among themselves, who **exchanged the truth of God** for the lie, and worshipped and served the creature rather than the Creator, who is blessed forever, Amen. For this reason God gave them up to vile passions. For even their women exchanged the natural use for what is against nature. Likewise also the men, leaving the natural use of the woman, burned in their lust for one another, men with men committing what is shameful, and receiving in themselves the penalty of their error which is due.*

God "gave them up" is a judicial term in Greek, used for handing over a prisoner to his or her sentence. When individuals or a people consistently abandon God, He will abandon them. He accomplishes this indirectly and immediately:

- By *removing His restraint* and allowing their sin to run its course.
- Directly and eventually by specific acts of divine judgment and punishment.

The United States has joined Europe and the rest of the West; it seems on a downward spiral of immorality. Our Western society does not want God as shown even in many churches as people continuously *reject the truth of His Word.* Choosing rather to accept and live the known lie. Father forgive us, and give us repentant hearts that we turn back to You. And have mercy on our leadership that they seek your wisdom. Don't leave us, I pray in Jesus' name, Amen.

If you are reading this and you have not accepted Christ as your Savior, "Why not do it now? Believe on the Lord Jesus, who loves you and gave His life for you. Jesus said, ***"I am the door. If anyone enters by Me, he [or she] will be saved" (see John 10:9).*** *Only* Jesus Christ is the *One true* source for the knowledge of God and the *One* basis for our authentic spiritual security.

What shall we believe?

On occasion, Jesus was asked, "What shall we do that we may work the works of God?" Jesus answered and said to them, "This is the work of God that you believe in Him whom He sent" (John 6:28-29). And the promise is that "whosoever believes in Him should not perish but have everlasting life" (see John 3:16). Like so many today, these people thought Jesus was saying that God required them to do some works to *earn* everlasting life, which they thought they would be able to do. We must believe that:

- Jesus is the Son of God, that He is able and willing to save us from sin and bestow the priceless gift of eternal life upon His followers.
- We must believe in Him as our *personal Savior,* that He died for *us,* and that His death on the cross was the penalty for *our sin,* which He paid on *our* behalf.
- Believing this, the next step is to repent of our sins, confessing them to Him, and then believe with all my heart that He forgives and cleanses, for *"if we confess our sins, He is faithful and just to forgive us our sins, and to cleanse us from all unrighteousness" (1 John 1:9).*

Let Christ save

Our part in receiving salvation is to accept wholeheartedly the fact that we can do nothing to save ourselves; Jesus Christ is able to save to the uttermost all that come unto God by Him. We are to surrender the matter entirely into Jesus' hands. Let *Him* save.

He gave His life on Calvary to obtain this privilege. *"Nor is there salvation in any other, for there is no other name under heaven given among men by which we must be saved" (Acts 4:12).*

Will you, then, come to Him and be saved? Your case is not too hard for Him. Your burden is not too heavy for Him to bear. Your sin is not too great for Him to fully pardon. He is able to save to the uttermost. His salvation is yours if you will only believe. Hear this loving invitation,

And the Spirit and the bride say,
"Come!"
And let him who hears say,
"Come!"
And let him who thirsts come.
Whosoever desires,
let him take the water
of life freely
(Revelation 22:17).

STUDY SUMMARY

CHAPTER 7

WHAT MUST I DO TO BE SAVED?

What question did the jailer ask Paul and Silas?

"What must I do to be saved?" (see Acts 16:30).

What was their answer?

"So they said, "Believe on the Lord Jesus Christ, and you will be saved, you and your household" (Acts 16:31).

Can a person save them self from the guilt and power of sin?

"For by grace you have been saved through faith, and that not of yourselves, it is the gift of God, not of works, lest anyone should boast (Ephesians 2:8-9).

Who can save a man?

"For unto you is born . . . . a Savior who is Christ the Lord" (Luke 2:11).

When a sinner is impressed by the Holy Spirit to forsake his or her sins, what is the first step to be taken?

"But without faith it is impossible to please Him, for he who comes to God must believe that He is, and that He is a rewarder of those who diligently seek Him." (Hebrews 11:6).

"I believe that You are the Christ, the Son of God, who is to come into the world" (John 11:27).

Does the devil try to hinder men and women from believing in God's power and Word?

"Then the devil comes and takes away the word out of their hearts, lest they should believe and be saved" (Luke 8:12).

After believing that Christ can save you, what is the next step?

"Repent, and believe in the gospel" (Mark 1:15).

Chapter 8

BORN TWICE

Those who are saved through the regeneration or new birth in Jesus Christ *are born twice.* A complete transformation takes place in their lives so they are no longer the same individuals. Though their name is the same, *spiritually* they are entirely changed. They have been **born again: the first time of the flesh and the second time of the Holy Spirit.**

This is conversion. While it is mysterious and we can't explain it nevertheless it is reality! The new birth is as real as the natural birth. Both the individual and those who know him or her are aware of the change. The new birth has to do with the new nature produced in your spirit by the Holy Spirit.

"I will give you a new heart and put a new spirit within you; I will take the heart of stone out of your flesh and give you a heart of flesh. I will put My Spirit within you and cause you to walk in My statutes, and you will keep My judgments and do them" (Ezekiel 36:26, 27).

At conversion the entire life is regenerated and changed. The old carnal desires, the tendency to sin, and the love of the world become subdued; and all replaced by a zeal to serve God and do right. Through the new birth men and women become "new creations." "Old things are passed away; behold all things are become new" (2 Corinthians 5:17). We also have the promise of God through the Apostle Paul, "If we walk in the Spirit; we **shall** *[used to indicate a promise, determination or a command]* **not** fulfill the lust of the flesh" (Galatians 5:16).

This is a critical area in the life of the young convert and therefore much teaching and mentoring is required. The potential of the flesh energized by Satan should in no way be underestimated. If given free rein the *flesh* will direct our *choices* making us do things we know we **should not** do. The *real* sin of Adam and Eve was the fact **they felt that they had a RIGHT to choose <u>to be and to act</u> relationally independent of God and whatever concerns Him!**

Six thousand years later this major sin continues to haunt humanity. In fact that same sin is becoming more and more prevalent in this country not only in the secular arena but also among God's people. Like Adam and Eve, there are those who knowingly choose the wrong over the right, a lie over truth, or evil over good. Yet, it's important that we realize that Adam and Eve's *sinful decision* has distorted every decision humankind has made since that day. Therefore, only through God can we know what is right and wrong. It does not come to us naturally; but must be spiritually revealed.

We are dependent upon God totally and we must keep Him in the center of each decision we make! The inner conflict between the flesh and the spirit is very *real*. It is evident that these people operating out of their sinful nature are not children of God. This is spiritual warfare in its truest sense. The Spirit desires that we be free from sin and God's children walk in the Spirit! Right, godly choices that bring fulfillment and joy to our lives are those that line up in proper relationship with the person and character of a holy, righteous God. He alone establishes the perimeters of right and wrong; and always in our best interest. Praise God!

A New Creation

It is strictly a miracle of God's grace that changes a sinner into a Christian. When it is completed the entire life is altered. He or she is a new creation. No longer **should** *[which expresses obligation, duty, or expectation]* **the works** of the flesh, such as adultery, fornication, uncleanness, lasciviousness, idolatry, witchcraft, hatred, variance, emulations, wrath, strife, seditions, heresies, envying, murder, drunkenness, reveling, and the like dominate your life. The Scripture admonishes, "Those who practice such things will not inherit the kingdom of God" (Galatians 5:19-21). The works of the flesh will fall away, when the life is regenerated by the Holy Spirit and lived by the Spirit.

Instead of the works of the flesh, the beautiful fruit of the Spirit begins to appear. The fruit is "love, joy, peace, long-suffering, gentleness, goodness, faith, meekness, temperance," for Paul says, "And those who are Christ's have crucified the flesh with its passions and desires. If we live in the Spirit, let us also walk in the Spirit" (Galatians 5:22-25).

The Scripture promises, *"He who overcomes shall be clothed in white garments, and I will not blot out his [her] name from the "Book of Life; but I will confess his[her] name before My Father and before His angels" (Revelation 3:5).* Brackets are mine. The new creation or Spirit-formation is absolutely necessary for Christian living. Paul expressed it, by nature, "There is none who does good no not one" (Romans 3:12).

The Lord writes the principles of His law upon this new heart and new nature; which is now susceptible to the influence and guidance. Men and women are no longer left to stumble in the darkness as he or she is now under the control of the Spirit of God, who, as Christ's personal representative, has taken up His abode inside to bring you to Christlikeness. In John 14:16, 17 Jesus promised,

"And I will pray the Father,
And He will give you another Helper,
That He may abide with you forever
The Spirit of truth,
Whom
The world cannot receive,
Because it neither
Sees Him nor knows Him, for He dwells
With you
And
Will be in you."

STUDY SUMMARY

CHAPTER 8

BORN TWICE

What takes place in the life of a sinner when he or she confesses their sins to God, accept Christ as the Savior, and believes that his or her sins are forgiven?

He or she is converted. "Repent therefore and be converted, that your sins may be blotted out, so that times of refreshing may come from the presence of the Lord" (Acts 3:19).

This means that this person's life is changed. He or she no longer owes their allegiance to Satan and sin, but now takes their place as a child of God.

What does God promise to write upon the new heart?

For this is the covenant that I will make with the house of Israel after those days, says the Lord: I will put My laws in their mind and write them on their hearts; and I will be their God and they shall be My people" (Hebrews 8:10).

What change is noticeable in the converted individual?

Instead of the works of the flesh, the fruit of the Spirit now appears: [love, joy, peace, gentleness, goodness, and faith]; as this disciple is spirit-formed.

How does Christ dwell in the hearts of men and women?

"That Christ may dwell in your hearts by faith" (Ephesians 3:17).

Chapter 9

JUSTIFIED BY FAITH

Keeping the Law of Moses did not free anyone from their sins. But the atoning death of Jesus completely satisfied the demands of God's law, making forgiveness of all sins available to all who believe. Only the forgiveness that Christ offers can free people from their sins. (see Romans 3:20, 23). In Acts 13:39, we read,

And by Him everyone
*who believes is **justified***
from all things
from which you could not be justified
by the law of Moses.

Justification means "declared righteous" and therefore righteous and acceptable to God. The blood of Jesus was the payment for our sin debt. The Lawgiver came to earth and became the Law Keeper. Christ obeyed every law perfectly; and accepts His full and free pardon for their transgressions.

- He imputes His righteousness to them.
- He did it in their name.
- When they accept Him as their substitute—He credits them His sinless life.
- He counts it as if they had always lived righteously rather than sinfully.
- That is "justification." His record stands in the place of their record.

Even the righteousness of God through faith in Jesus Christ to all and on all who believe. For there is no difference; for all have sinned and fall short of the glory of God, being justified freely by His grace through the redemption that is in Christ Jesus, whom God set forth as a propitiation by His blood, through faith, to demonstrate His *righteousness, because in His forbearance God had passed over sins that were previously committed, to demonstrate at the present time His righteousness, that He might be just and the justifier of the one who has faith in Jesus* (Romans 3:22-26). Paul gives two reasons why the righteousness of God comes through Jesus' death:

- The first is to *demonstrate* that God Himself is righteous, and did not judge the sins committed prior to the cross.
- The second reason for the cross is that God wanted to *show* that He is both righteous and at the same time the *One* who can declare sinners righteous.

Because of Christ's death, God does not compromise His holiness when He forgives a sinner. The law could only condemn them, but God was the One who saved them. Therefore, we owe Him all of our praise and glory.

Whosoever Will

God is no respecter of persons. God is so good! The most hardened sinner can find grace equally with the person whose sins seem much lighter. His invitation is, *"Whosoever will, may come."* If they will only come, He promises He will in no wise cast them out. Those who come are cleansed because of what Christ has done for them. Speaking through the prophet, Jesus said, *"I will cleanse them from all their iniquity by which they have sinned against Me, and I will pardon all their iniquities by which they have sinned and by which they have transgressed against Me" (Jeremiah 33:8).*

For as the heavens are high above the earth, so great is His mercy toward those who fear Him; as far as the east is from the west, so far has He removed our transgressions from us (Psalm 103:11-12). ". . . . The blood of Jesus Christ His Son cleanses us from all sin" (1 John 1:7). Thus giving back to us what Adam and Eve lost in Eden, making it possible for imperfect believers to have fellowship with a holy God.

Forgiven and Forgotten

Notice, the promises continue, *"I will forgive their iniquity, and their sin I will remember no more." (Jeremiah 31:34b).* Notice, God does not hold on to the record of the repentant sinner's debts and sins for which Christ died. The account has been fully settled, and marked "PAID!" Wow! What an astounding message this is! "I will remember their sin no more." He has cast them "into the depth of the sea" (Micah 7:19), from which they shall never rise to condemn the faithful believer.

God's appeal is to every individual. "Look to Me and be saved, all you ends of the earth! For I am God, and there is no other" (Isaiah 45:22). His invitation to all humanity to come to Jesus for pardon and complete justification is universal to all. His nail-scarred hands are outstretched today lovingly bidding all to come and be saved. The death of Jesus was surely for each sinner—as it would have been for if only one sinner alone. Sinners everywhere are the object of His love and tender care. The Lord declares, "I have loved you with an everlasting love; therefore with loving-kindness I have drawn you" (Jeremiah 31:3).

Adopted into the Family of God

The standard definition of adoption for most of us is the act of taking voluntarily a child of other parents as one's own child; in a theological sense, the act of God's grace by which sinful people are brought into God's redeemed family. However, Lockyer's Illustrated Dictionary of the Bible adds that in the New Testament times, Roman custom exercised a great deal of influence on Jewish family life. One custom is particularly significant in relation to adoption.

Roman law required that the adopter be a male and childless; the one to be adopted had to be an independent adult, able to *agree* to be adopted. In the eyes of the law, the adopted one became a *new creature;* and was regarded as being *born again* into the new family, an illustration of what happens to the believer at conversion.

The Apostle Paul used this legal concept of adoption as an analogy to show the believer's relationship to God. Although similar ideas are found throughout the New Testament, the word adoption, used in a theological sense, is found only in Paul's writings (see Romans 8:15, 23; 9:4). In Ephesians, Paul's emphasis was that our adoption rests with God who had already decided [predestined] to make us His own children through Jesus Christ (Ephesians 1:5 NCV). In his letter to the Romans, Paul used the term to describe Israel's place of honor in God's plan (Romans 9:4).

However, Gentile believers have also been given the *"Spirit of adoption,"* who brings them to *maturity*, to *full* son-ship which allows them to cry, "Abba, Father" (Galatians 4:6). In new birth, God has sent forth the Spirit of His Son into your hearts; and with this baptism of the Spirit, he or she receives the first fruits, earnest and seal of the Spirit. The Spirit of adoption transforms the believer's spirit through the Word of God from a spiritual slave to being a son [daughter] with *full* rights and privileges. Also this blessing carries a future dimension, the assurance that the believer's body will be resurrected (Romans 8:23).

Some Results of Adoption

Note some of the results of adoption on the human side.

- We have the family name (see Ephesians 3:14, 15; 1 John 3:1; Revelation 2:17; 3:12).
- We have the family likeness (see Colossians 3:10; Romans 8:29; II Corinthians 3:18).
- We have the parents' nature (see II Peter 1:4; John 1:12, 13; 3:6).
- We have the family love (see 1 John 2:9-11; 3:14-18; 4:7-8; 5:1).

Note some of the results of adoption on the Divine side:

- We are the objects of God's peculiar love (see John 17:22-23; 16:27).
- We are the subjects of God's care (see Matthew 6:32).
- We are the subjects of God's paternal discipline (see Hebrews 12:6-11).
- We are the subjects of God's paternal comfort (see II Corinthians 1:4).
- We are made heirs to an inheritance (see I Peter 1:2-5; Romans 8:17).

The Lord Jesus was revealed as the Son of God, a *mature* Son, at John's baptism in the Jordan (see Matthew 3:17). A true son [or daughter] of God will walk as Christ walked in this world. He or she will hate sin, live righteously, and love the brethren (see I John 2:6; 4:17). Christ the Son will live His life in His sons. The Son of God became the Son of man that the sons of men might become the sons of God. The New Testament writers refer to various stages of spiritual formation [of the believer's adoption into sonship] and uses them to encourage the believer to grow up into maturity (see 1 John 2:12-14).

Regeneration	Adoption
Born of the Spirit	Matured by the Spirit
As a child	As a son
Immature	Matured
Ernest of inheritance	Full inheritance
First fruits of the Spirit	Fullness of the Spirit
Witness of the Spirit	Possessed of the Spirit
Spirit of Adoption	Adoption realized
Subject to sin and death	Redemption of the body
As a servant	As a son perfect and mature
Discipline and obedience	Character and privileges
Made heirs	Receives the inheritance

In regeneration the believer is born again, as a child into the family of God (see John 1:12-13; 3:3-5).

- This has to do with *relationship* rather than position.
- This is the imparting of a *new nature* and is "son-making."
- In adoption the regenerated believer, at the age of maturity, is placed as a son. This has to do with *position* and *privileges* rather than *relationship*.
- This is "son-placing" (see Galatians 4:1-2).

In regeneration, one receives *new life*. In justification one receives *new standing*. In adoption one receives a *new position*. Adoption has to do with the legal status as a son or [daughter] being given *full rights of inheritance* which concludes at the coming of Christ. (see 1 John 3:1; Romans 8:23).

STUDY SUMMARY

CHAPTER 9

JUSTIFIED BY FAITH

What is meant by the doctrine of justification?

To justify means to declare one innocent who has been guilty. It is a gracious act of God; wherein God imputes to him or her His own righteousness and declares before the whole world that the sinner is guiltless.

Who may be justified?

Everyone, who believes in Jesus Christ as His or her Savior and is willing to accept His righteousness, *"By everyone who believes is justified from all things" (see Acts 13:39).*

Who has sinned?

For *all* have sinned and fall short of the glory of God (Romans 3:23).

How do repentant sinners receive Christ's righteousness?

It is a *gift* from God. *"Therefore, as through one man's offense judgment came to all men, resulting in condemnation, even so through one Man's righteous act the free gift came to all men, resulting in justification of life. For as by one man's disobedience many were made sinners, so also by one Man's obedience many will be made righteous." (Romans 5:18, 19).*

How does one receive justification from God?

"Therefore we conclude that a man is justified by faith apart from the deeds of the law." (Romans 3:28). It is by faith! The sinner

must ask for pardon and cleansing; but he or she must believe that God will grant the request.

What does God promise to those who are clothed with the righteousness of Christ?

"They shall walk with Me in white, for they are worthy. He who overcomes shall be clothed in white garments, and I will not blot out his name from the Book of Life; but I will confess his name before My Father and before His angels" (see Revelation 3:4, 5).

What happens when the believers are adopted?

They are given full rights of inheritance which concludes at the coming of Jesus.

SECTION IV

Give Me Jesus

Chapter 10

I'VE GOT TO HAVE JESUS!

Up to this point in God's story concerning man's redemption, I have attempted to emphasize God's plan of reconciling man back to Himself through salvation beginning with [justification and adoption]. As discussed in chapter nine, the Apostle Paul used the Roman model of legal adoption as an analogy to show the believer's relationship to God. There the one to be adopted [in our case, the spiritual believer] had to be an independent adult [able to agree]. Similar to the parable of the Sower, the success of the entire process is dependent upon a thorough [good ground] Spirit induced understanding of the revealed truth of God's Word. Carefully study the six references below and depend on the Holy Spirit to lead you to the revealed truths:

1. The Gospel—I Corinthians 15:1
2. Given the Spirit of adoption—Romans 8:15; Ephesians 1:5
3. New creature—II Corinthians 5:17
4. Born again into the family of God—John 3:3
5. Responsibility to grow up into maturity—II Peter 1:3
6. Realize our full inheritance—Ephesians 1:11; I Peter 1:4

Profession not Confession

In many churches today, the salvation experience is equated to applying for church membership. The individual simply comes forth at the invitation and the church clerk or equivalent will have them fill out a membership form containing their personal data.

The information given on the form becomes the means of salvation, because in many instances that is the extent of the requirements for membership. This process receives many on the profession [not confession] of their faith; baptism may or may not be performed or excluded [lack of facility]. Not only is the gospel muddled in this instance, but the fine points of salvation as in the examples of revealed truth above are also neglected.

America has fallen right into Satan's deception of success in numbers and size, or some "other way" to God other than through the authentic Jesus Christ, who is the only Way! The multicultural landscape of America has introduced many gods, which has brought idolatry and hedonism to an all-time high. Idolatry primarily involves allowing anything or anyone to stand in the place of God. Our society has come to rely so heavily on permissiveness, technology and government to solve its problems that many people no longer feel a need for God. Also there are those who attempt to use Him only in conjunction with their physical needs just as another source of relief.

Satan is striving to make it normal to place as much or more faith in human ingenuity as god; just as the ancient Babylonians placed in their ingenuity and carved images. Additionally, psychotherapies practically do away with any need for the God of the Bible. Instead, they rely on their own principles and methods to deal with guilt and sin, supposedly to make people whole [limited at best through treatment, since only God heals]. They declare even amidst the unfavorable evidence of the opposite, that people can become all that they were meant to be without God. To our shame, much of this is spouted today from the nation's pulpits. Then there is the everyday idolatry seen through television and films which glamorize occult practices using physical objects, séances, supposedly good witches, warlords, and crystals to tell fortunes and receive supernatural messages. Though more sophisticated than the Babylonian shrines set up to pagan gods, it is still idolatry. Satan also presses for the theory of evolution to replace the first eleven chapters of the Bible as the origin of humanity. While the prophecies of such notables as Ezekiel on Satan's origin; and Isaiah speaking for God in the text below are for the most part neglected or dismissed today leaving spiritually blind people ignorant to the essential need or place for the truths of God's Word concerning the authentic Jesus Christ in their lives. [God forbid!]. In order for America's end to have meaning, leadership at all levels must as ancient Israel did, go back and take note of the beginning. God declares,

---

"Remember the former things of old, for I am God, and there is no other; I am God, and there is none like Me, [declaring the end from the beginning], and from ancient times [things that are not yet done]. Saying My counsel shall stand, and I will do all My pleasure" (Isaiah 46:9-10).

The Book of II Kings records in chapter 17, a period wherein Israel, while worshipping God continued to serve their idols. God hates that! It's like jogging on a treadmill while eating a couple of glazed doughnuts, demonstrating against the killing of animals for food, but pro-abortion! What so-called innocent forms of idolatry are you keeping and passing on? The first and second Commandments are as valid today as when they were written by the finger of God (see Exodus 20:2-6). Likewise, the Lord is still who He declared Himself to be to the ancients: "I am God, and there is no other; I am God, and there is none like Me" (Isaiah 46:9).

Humankind must realize that man and woman were created for the glory of God and relationship with Him in community. The perfect example of this relationship and community [fellowship] is pictured as God came down and walked in perfect relationship with Adam and Eve in the Garden of Eden. Satan through the introduction of sin caused the break up of that fellowship, thus separating Adam and Eve from God. This left humanity with absolutely no way in their power of reconciling with God. If reconciliation was to happen, God would have to institute it. God promised a remedy for man's predicament in Genesis 3:15,

"And I will put enmity
Between you and the woman,
And between your seed and her Seed;
He shall bruise your head,
And you shall bruise His heel."

Satan bruised Jesus' heel at Calvary; but he by no means took His life. Jesus laid down His life in order to provide *the way* of reconciliation with God, the Father. If we are to be reconciled to the Father, like Christ, we must lay down our lives; which is accomplished through regeneration.

For when we were still without strength, in due time Christ died for the ungodly. For scarcely for a righteous man will one die; yet perhaps for a good man someone would even dare to die. But **God demonstrates His own love toward us,** *in that while we were still sinners, Christ died for us. Much more then, having now been justified* **by His blood, we shall be saved** *from wrath through Him. For if when we were enemies* **we were reconciled to God through the death of His Son,** *much more, having been reconciled,* **we shall be saved by His life.** *And not only that, but we also rejoice in God* **through our Lord Jesus Christ,** *through whom we have now received the reconciliation (Romans 5:6-11).*

If God loved us when we were helpless, ungodly enemies, how much more will He love us now that we are His children? By His blood through the death of His Son we have been **justified,** that is [declared righteous], and **reconciled,** [meaning our alienation from God has been changed]. Believers are no longer at war with God. **They are at peace with Him!** Think back to the relationship and fellowship that Adam had with God prior to sin. Adam and Eve could communicate [expression, understanding and language] with God. They were in community. God supplied their every need [He gave them Paradise for their home]. If they had a question about anything they could turn to God, their Creator for the answer.

They were innocent and totally dependent upon Him for their very existence. His unconditional love was all they knew and all they needed to know. Then came sin!

The point is that since God's love and the death of Christ have brought us *justification*, this righteousness imputed to us by Almighty God through Jesus Christ His Son brings the following seven results which summarize verses 1-11:

- **We have peace with God (v. 1)**—not by works (4:1-8), not by ordinances (4:9-12), not by obedience to the Law (4:13-22)—but *"by faith, we have peace with God through Jesus Christ . . . ."* (v. 1). Christ Jesus Himself ***"is our peace"*** (see Ephesians 2:14). "A Happy Day" it is when you accept the fact that all God has to offer you is Jesus! *"You are complete in Him" (Colossians 2:10).*

Give me Jesus—the Authentic Christ!

- **We have access into grace (v. 2)**—*"by faith into this grace wherein we stand . . . ."* The word *"access"* literally means "a way in." Jesus clothes the believer with Himself and His righteous, cleanses him or her in His own precious blood, and brings them into the unlimited favor and infinite grace of the Father. All humans are shutout from God's presence; and there is absolutely no way for man or woman to approach God and hope to gain audience with Him—**except through the Lord Jesus Christ.** Jesus said, ***"I am the Door: by Me if any man [woman] enter in, he [she] shall be saved, and shall go in and out, and find pasture" (John 10:9).*** Again to Thomas He said, ***"I am the Way, the Truth, and the Life: no man [woman] comes unto the Father, but by Me" (John 14:6).*** [Brackets are mine]. By Him "we have access by faith." The Gospel has been preached and whosoever receives and stands on it is saved (see 1

Corinthians 15:1). We who are saved have been *"accepted in the Beloved" (see Ephesians 1:6).* Positionally, we ***"are dead, and our life is hid with Christ in God"*** (see Colossians 3:3). *In Jesus* we are **righteous and holy** (see II Corinthians 5:21).

- **We rejoice in the hope of the glory of God (v. 2).** The believer, knowing the peace of God because Jesus has ***"made peace through the blood of His cross" (Colossians 1:20),*** has the right to *"rejoice in hope"* because Jesus has opened for him or her a way into God's presence, fellowship, and peace. Oh! How precious and exciting to know that *now* we sit together in heavenly places in Christ Jesus; to know that our lives are hid with Christ in God. It is certainly "joy unspeakable and full of glory" (1 Peter 1:8).

- **We glory in tribulations (vv. 3-5).** As believers we do not glory only in the fact that we are saved and know that we are at peace with God; we rejoice in tribulation—*"knowing that tribulation produces perseverance, and perseverance, character; and character, hope." Now, hope does not disappoint (vv. 3-5).* A hope that is sure that "all things work together for good to those who love God, to those who are the called according to His purpose" (Romans 8:28). Today, too many Christians are throwing up their hands and quitting at the first sign of trials denoting a deficiency in their spiritual formation.

- **God's love is shed abroad in our hearts (v. 5a).** The love of God referred to in this verse in not our love for God—but it is *God's own love [agape]* as it pours forth from **His great heart <u>through our heart!</u>** The *indwelling love of God is proof that we are saved.* Love is the very essence of salvation: *"You are of God, little children, and have overcome them,* **because He who is in you is greater than he who is in the world.** *Beloved, let us love one another, for love is of God;* and ***everyone who loves*** is ***born of God and knows God.***

Love for fellow believers is evidence that one has passed from the realm of death to the sphere of life!

*He who **does not love, does not know God, for God is love.** No one has seen God at any time; **if we love one another, God abides in us,** and **His love has been perfected in us.** And we have known and believed the love that God has for us. God is love, and he who abides in love abides in God and God in him (I John 4: 7, 8, 12, 16).*

- *Love is the fruit of the Spirit (see Galatians 5:22).* We know He lives within us because of the presence of God's love in our hearts. Today it seems a new norm, even among believers to shun people because of their wicked lifestyles, evil ways, or negative manners. If we willingly submit completely to the love of God, God will love them through us in spite of our weakness through the flesh. If that is your condition and you are willing to allow God to love that person through you, He will work a miracle in your life. *"It is God who works in you both to will and to do for His good pleasure" (Philippians 2:13).* In **(vv. 6-10)** we are led to the seventh result of justification (v. 11).

- **We rejoice in God (v. 11).** The believer has been brought into a new state of reconciliation, and certainly God will keep him or her there. Therefore we "rejoice in God." We not only enjoy the blessings of God, but actually believers by position are in God (see Colossians 3:3). Being *reconciled* to God changes the relationship between God and us. Before becoming believers we were enemies with God; but now reconciled, we rejoice in God; and this rejoicing in God is ours, through our Lord and Savior, Jesus Christ, by whom we have now received the atonement. Our salvation is by faith in the finished work of the Lord Jesus Christ. Salvation is dependent upon the promise given in the Word of God, *"As many as received Him, to them He* *gave power to become the sons of God, even to them that believe on His name"* which were born, not of blood, nor of the will of the flesh, nor of the will of man, but of God" (John 1:12, 13).

Today people are grasping for truth and depending on preaching and teaching to bring them into reality through application of the truths in their lives. In many instances, they are finding only more disappointment as they are led into thinking applications; which are taught to be naturally acquired when in fact; they can only be meaningfully acquired and applied through the Spirit.

STUDY SUMMARY

CHAPTER 10

I'VE GOT TO HAVE JESUS!

We hear of the gospel in song, jazz gospel, gospel plays, hip hop gospel, country gospel, and rock gospel—what is the definition of the gospel according to the Scripture?

The fifteenth chapter of I Corinthians is called the "Resurrection chapter" because it is the most extensive treatment of the subject in the Bible. It follows then, that the gospel defined is recorded by Paul in chapter 15: *"I delivered unto you first of all that which I also received: that Christ died for our sins according to the Scriptures, and that He was buried, and that He rose again the third day according to the Scriptures."*

Where is the promise of a Redeemer for humankind first mentioned in the Bible?

In Genesis 3:15: *"And I will put enmity between you and the woman, and between your seed and her Seed; He shall bruise your head, and you shall bruise His heel."*

All humans are shut-out from God's presence; and there is absolutely no way for any human being to approach God and hope to gain audience with Him—except through the Lord Jesus Christ. Jesus said, *"I am the Door: by Me if any man [or woman] enter in, he [or she] shall be saved, and shall go in and out, and find pasture" (John 10:9).* Again He said, *"I am the Way, the Truth, and the Life: no man [woman] comes to the Father, but by Me" (John 14:6).* Brackets are mine throughout.

How can the Christian rejoice in tribulation?

"Knowing that tribulation produces perseverance, and perseverance, character; and character, hope. Now hope does not disappoint" (1 Peter 1:3-5; also see Romans 8:28).

Is love for fellow believers an evidence that we have passed from death unto life?

Yes. *"The Scripture says, "Beloved, let us love one another, for love is of God; and everyone who loves is born of God and knows God. He who does not love does not know God, for God is love. No one has seen God at any time. If we love one another, God abides in us, and His love has been perfected in us. And we have known and believed the love that God has for us. God is love, and he who abides in love abides in God, and God in him"* (I John 4:7, 8, 12, 16).

Chapter 11

THE STRUGGLE IN THE
CHRISTIAN'S LIFE

I often think of the contrast in the relationship between Jesus and the Apostle John during Jesus' earthly walk, and their meeting years later on the Isle of Patmos. John called the beloved disciple, is often pictured with his head upon Christ's chest. They walked together for three years in ministry. However, when John met Him on Patmos—he fainted! Jesus walked no more after the flesh. As Jesus was last seen in the flesh [natural body] formed the lasting impression the world has of Jesus. He was the suffering Servant [bodily sacrificed] on the cross. Notice the difference in John's reaction when he turned and saw the glorified Christ on Patmos, *"I fell at His feet as dead"* (Revelation 1:17).

Sadly, the image the world holds of Christ is only seen in the humble, suffering Man of Galilee; which ended with their last glimpse of Him in death on the Cross. Since it is forbidden for Christians to strike or make images of Jesus Christ depicting His human form; that leaves it to the world. So for centuries, the world has commercialized drawings, paintings and images from their *last* visual scene of Him on earth [in death on the cross] otherwise all they have left to go on is their imagination. My wife and I attended a worship service some time ago wherein at a certain point the lighting was gradually extinguished; a spotlight gradually came on in a front corner of the church; the shape of a person could be seen approaching from the shadows into the evolving light. Suddenly, he was in the full light, the congregation gasped, "That's Jesus!" No, it was an actor dressed and made up to resemble the popular painting most of us have seen at some point in our lives. We find these images in some religious practices and even in our Christian homes. This innocent looking deception keeps many Christians from moving their spiritual gaze upward from Calvary and seeing in the Spirit as John did, the Jesus of Patmos, the authentic Christ, now seated at the right hand of the Father and functioning in His High Priestly role interceding for us! Yes, we are still in our earthly bodies, but praise God we should no longer walk after the flesh we are "in Him."

A good analogy of being "in Christ" is to be "in an airplane" at 33,000 feet up in the air traveling at 600 MPH. You are in the plane and safe from all of the elements, dangers, and sure death outside. In Christ you are safe from all of Satan's elements and sure death.

In Christ

Like John on Patmos, Paul speaks of our relationship [in Christ] as different from that of an earthly relationship. In II Corinthians 5:17, He states, "If anyone is in Christ he [or she] is a new creation; old things have passed away; behold, all things have become new." Our perspective moves from earthly to a heavenly outlook. Through the truth of this verse we see that:

- When Christ died on Calvary's cross—the believer died with Him.
- When Jesus rose from the dead and walked out of the tomb, every born again believer rose from the dead with Him; therefore, we should live not to ourselves, but unto the Lord Jesus Christ, in whom we died when He died and rose again with Him when He rose from the dead.

- The Christ we now know is not a Babe in a manger; He is not the Man of Galilee; He is not the Christ nailed to a cross or lying in a tomb. *The Christ we now know is seated at the right hand of God the Father.* No, No, He is not the Christ according to the flesh [He is the same Christ in a sense] but He is not now in the body in which He conquered the world, the flesh, and the devil, and in which He fulfilled the Law. He is now seated in His resurrected body making intercession for us, pleading our case before a Holy God (see Hebrews 7:35). We will have a glorious body like His when we meet Him in the first resurrection. Give Him praise and glory.

- **These eternal Bible truths must be taught, caught and emphasized today as never before. Christ is alive and ruling!** The world promotes the Jesus of Galilee as I stated above, because that's how it last saw Him. Oh, but saints we have a much higher view of Him! Peter declared, ". . . . God has made Him both Lord and Christ" (see Acts 2:42-36). Paul said, "God also has highly exalted, and given Him a name which is above every name . . . . that every tongue should confess that Jesus Christ is the Lord to the glory of God the Father" (Philippians 2:9-11).

- Confession of the Lordship of Jesus is necessary for salvation (see Romans 10:9-13; 1 Corinthians 12:3; Acts 9:1-6).

- The name, Lord Jesus Christ is the greatest redemptive name ever to be revealed.

The significance of the believer's redemption includes the following:

- The believer's security is in Christ; who bore in His body God's judgment against sin.
- The believer's acceptance is in Christ with whom God is well-pleased.

- The believer's future acceptance is with Christ who is the resurrection to eternal life and the sole guarantor of our inheritance in heaven.
- The believer's participation in the divine nature of Christ, the everlasting Word (see 2 Peter 1:4).
- In salvation Christ gave the believer His righteousness which includes not only justification, but also sanctification (see 2 Corinthians 5:21).

Sanctification (Spiritual formation)

After receiving justification, Christians should live **holy** lives that reflect the divine nature of God [given in regeneration] who saved them. Because it is written, ***"Be holy, for I am holy" (1 Peter 1:16).*** He or she should *separate* themselves from actions, influences, or people that will contaminate them. Further, they should apply the biblical principles of *spiritual formation* [allowing the Spirit to form you into Christlikeness and to avoid what is:

- Against a biblical standard of purity legislated by Government or any other method (see 1 Corinthians 6:17-20; II Corinthians 10:4-5).
- Against a biblical prohibition (see Exodus 20:3-17).
- An association that will harm (see II Corinthians 6:14-18).
- Harmful to the body (see I Corinthians 6:19).
- Harmful to a weaker brother (see I Corinthians 8:8-13).
- Offensive to the conscience (see James 4:17).
- Failure to follow the example of Christ (see 1 Peter 2:21).

Sanctification [holiness] [saints] essentially defines the Christian's new Spirit-formed nature and conduct in contrast with the pre-salvation lifestyle. We practice a holy manner of living because we are associated with the Holy God and must treat Him and His Word with reverence and respect. We therefore glorify Him best by being like Him (study 1 Peter 1:15-21).

Sanctification is activated by love. In verse 22, Peter admonishes, *"Since you have purified your souls in obeying the truth through the Spirit in sincere love of the brethren, love one another fervently with a pure heart."* The love spoken of by Peter here is the love of choice, the kind of love that responds to a command. "Fervently" in this passage denote "without limits." Only those whose souls have been saved and Spirit formed have the capacity to love like this. This love lends itself to meeting others at their point of need. What the Christians need *to be* and the world needs *to see* in them is the authentic Christ manifested in what we *are* (holy) and what we *do* (service). I've used these words *holy, sanctified* and I will now add *saints* interchangeably because they are all translated from the same root word for holiness. Notice how Paul describes the church at Corinth in *two* different ways.

> *To the church of God which is at Corinth,*
> *to those who are **sanctified** in Christ Jesus,*
> *called to be **saints**,*
> *with all who in every place*
> *call on the name of Jesus Christ our Lord.*
> *(I Corinthians 1:2)*

1. They are **"sanctified** in Christ Jesus," which means they have been spirit-formed into Christlikeness by the Spirit, in Christ through His death and resurrection.
2. They are "called to be **saints.**"

It is important here to recognize that when Paul writes that these Corinthian Christians are called to be saints, he doesn't mean that they are to *grow* into saints, or become saints at some point in the future. Paul means, the Corinthian Christians *are* saints!" What this passage is teaching is:

- Holiness begins with your act of trusting the Lord Jesus Christ as your personal Savior.
- At that moment, you become a saint and sanctified. Does that necessarily mean that your ensuing behavior reflects what is true about you? Absolutely not!
- The church at Corinth, that Paul referred to as "those who are sanctified in Christ Jesus," who are "called to be saints" received a strong rebuke from Paul. Just a couple of pages over, he delivered his strong rebuke concerning many of their sins, including gross immorality, widespread divisions, and bitter envy.

This church at Corinth was probably the most *"carnal"* church in the New Testament (see I Corinthians 3:3). Yet as you read through both I and II Corinthians, he doesn't invite them to, or suggest they become saints but rather *to change their behavior!* He does not tell them that because of their *"unsaintly"* behavior they can no longer be saints. Instead he argues because they *are* saints—*they should **live as** saints!*

The Bible does not obscure it: The unsaved can only live like sinners; that's what they are. However, Christians are saints who may choose to live like sinners for a period of time. If Christians live like sinners, we must confront them and challenge them to repent and depend on the Holy Spirit to deliver them. They are then to walk in holiness.

All believers have been sanctified—but not all believers live sanctified lives.

Many Scripture passages support this position, including 1 Peter 2:9-11, which fully supports much of what I am attempting to clarify at this juncture. Notice: *But you **are** a chosen generation, a royal priesthood, a **holy nation**, His own special people, that you may proclaim the praises of Him who called out of darkness into the marvelous light; who once were not a people but **are now the people of God,** who had not obtained mercy but now have obtained. Beloved, I beg you as sojourners and pilgrims **abstain from fleshly lusts** which war against the soul.*

Peter said these people had accepted Christ as their personal Savior; they were brought "out of darkness into His marvelous light." Without a doubt they had been born again and were therefore *saints,* having been *sanctified.* So why does Peter have to "beg" them to "abstain from fleshly lusts?" Because they were indulging in fleshly lusts and sinning against the Lord! Where the Spirit is leading us with this is evident: The sanctification that occurs because of the *belief* in the finished work of Jesus does not, in and of itself, equate to holiness in the *behavior* of the believer.

The sanctification that occurs because of the belief in the finished work of Jesus does not in and of itself—equate to holiness in the behavior of the believer.

So, how can we be called holy when our behavior does not reflect holiness? I'm sure we see, the essence of justification isn't in the change of the behavior of the person, it's a change in the mind of God about that person. At the moment of conversion, the person *(not the behavior)* becomes holy, a saint in the eyes of God, is supernaturally *separated* to Himself. This aspect of the Christian life needs special attention today because many even in church leadership are beginning to accept "un-saintly behavior" as a norm. Certainly to do so not only weakens the church, but it deceives the weak Christian by allowing him or her to live a defeated life. Many words such as moral, integrity, character, commitment, loyalty, virtues and many other expressions and concepts that set the Christian apart unto God are being stricken from the church's vocabulary and substituted or redefined with words from the world's dictionary such as, inclusive of [any and everything including immorality], the new tolerance, which states that *[all truth is relative and therefore there can be no absolute or objective truth]*, and secular values [over biblical virtues]. This along with Satan's mind-games: head knowledge over biblical revelation knowledge, reason over wisdom, and inclusivity over exclusivity, erotic love (eros), and brotherly love (phileo) over unconditional love (agape). Those who embrace these changes support a secular worldview and therefore the secular agenda. [For a more in depth study see my book: *How Should We then Live*]. The Scriptures invite all people to come to Jesus just as they are; however, they certainly do not expect them to remain as they are! The Apostle Peter admonishes all believers to *"grow in grace and the knowledge of our Lord and Savior, Jesus Christ"* (2 Peter 3:18). Spiritual formation is expected of all saints (thoroughly study Romans 12:1-5; 2 Peter 1:1-9).

Holiness means Separation

Holiness has been defined by individuals and denominations in many ways, from the emotional experience, a certain dress (color or style), meditation, to food choices. However, we see God's idea of holiness in the "burning bush and holy ground" experience of Moses. In Exodus 3:3-5, God commanded Moses to take his shoes off because the ground on which he stood was *"holy ground."* In answering the question, *"How could this ground be holy?"* We also answer the question from the last segment, *"How can we be called holy when our behavior does not reflect holiness?"* The ground became holy simply because God *separated* it as the unique place where He would reveal Himself to Moses. Therefore, the ground was declared holy because God said it was holy. Moses comprehending God's command, simply obeyed Him. So to Moses the ground is holy in his thinking and understanding:

- Holiness requires *revelation.* The fundamental nature of [that spot] of ground did not change—but no one would have known the ground was "holy" unless God *revealed* it to him. [God said the ground was holy; so Moses acted upon His Word **by faith**, took his shoes off and stepped over onto holy ground]. Holy because God said it was holy!

- Holiness requires *separation* from one thing and *separation* to a different thing. It is obvious then, **"that you can't have one without the other."** For the ground to be holy it had to be *separated from* the rest of the desert and *separated to* God's presence and purpose.

- Holiness requires *disconnection*. For a person to become holy in this sense he or she must **depart from anything unholy—or holiness is impossible.**

- Holiness requires *reconnection.* For a person to become holy he or she must become **united and devoted to God.**

- Holiness requires *putting off and putting on.* New friends and acquaintances, new practices, and new pursuits [might require a career change] must be added to your life to **replace old unholy practices and patterns.**

- Holiness requires us to *abandon our unholy ways and pursue His holy ways.* Without **both aspects of this separation,** biblical holiness is impossible.

This is a person-to-person call that the Lord has placed to you. He is calling you to be holy. He beckons you to come out from all conduct and behavior that is inappropriate and be separated unto Him and devote yourself wholly to Him. Holiness is the center of God's will for His children. He wants you to be holy (see 1 Peter 1:15-16). Paul admonishes, *"That they may come to their senses and escape the snare of the devil, having been taken captive by him to do his will"* (2 Timothy 2:16).

Being Real

The Apostle Paul spoke of a situation in Romans 7 that is ruining the church in many quarters today. He said: *For what I am doing, I do not understand.* ***"For what I will to do, that I do not*** *practice; but what I hate that I do . . . ." For I know that in me (that is, in my flesh) nothing good dwells; for to will is present with me, but how to perform what is good I do not find.* **"For the good that I will to do, I do not do; but the evil I will not to do, that I practice.** *Now if I do what I will not to do,* **it is no longer I who does it, but sin that dwells in me"** **(Romans 7:15-20).** [Emphasis is mine].

In verse 14, Paul exclaims, "but I am carnal, sold under sin. Many try to explain away the possibility that he is actually discussing his own personal experiences in chapter 7. I believe that he did experience this carnal state. Perhaps those years of preparation in the desert with God brought him to the truth of the matter as he explained in chapter 8. Paul had a lot of head knowledge about the Law, but God had to teach him *heartfelt* grace and mercy. Throughout the Bible we find that most men whom God used had to wrestle with this problem of carnality. In his explanation of carnality Paul discovers two laws operating within.

- I delight in the *"law of God"* according to the "inner man."
- But I see another law in "my members," warring against the law of my mind, and bringing me into captivity to the *"law of sin"* which is in my members.

Before we can be an effective Christian in the service of our Lord, living a sanctified life of holiness; this warring in our minds must be settled [every entity in its proper place and order]. Before we were saved the law of sin; which we inherited from father Adam ruled in us; and thoroughly permeated our very members. Paul said, "I hate it, but I do it!" That cry is heard throughout the church today. Those who teach that this man or woman in this Romans 7 syndrome is *unsaved* are doing a great disservice to their churches. By allowing this cancer to continue to grow, we rob the church of its main ingredient, holiness. In fact this belief is allowing sinning [carnal Christians] to operate in all areas of the local church including the top leadership positions. I don't think we have to worry to much about the unsaved [natural man] in this instance. No! No! This individual delights in the law of God, the Holy Bible. This person is also knowledgeable of God and desires to please Him fully. Notice what Paul has to say in Romans 5-6 leading up to Romans 7:

*Therefore, as through one man's offense **judgment** came to all men, resulting in **condemnation**, even so through one Man's righteous act **the free gift came** to all men, resulting in **justification of life**. For as by **one man's disobedience** many were made **sinners**, so also by **one Man's obedience** many will be made **righteous**. Moreover the law entered that the offense might abound. **But where sin abounded, grace abounded much more,** so that as **sin reigned in death,** even so **grace might reign through righteousness to eternal life through Jesus Christ our Lord.** (Romans 5:18-21).*

- Adam's **sin** brought universal death, exactly the opposite of the result he expected and Satan had promised: "You will be like God" (Genesis 3:5).
- Christ's **sacrifice** brought salvation to those who believed.
- Adam brought upon all men the **condemnation** [the divine guilty verdict] for only one offense, his willful act of disobedience.
- Unlike Adam's act, Christ's act has accomplished and will accomplish exactly what He intended (see Philippians 1:6; Ephesians 2:5).
- Christ's death on the cross brought the **"the free gift"** **[salvation]** to all men and women who will exercise faith in Jesus Christ (see Romans 10:9-10).

Knowing this, that our old man was crucified with **Him,** that the body of sin might be done away with, that we **should** no longer be slaves of sin (Romans 6:6).

- Shall we continue in sin? Paul shouts, "Certainly not!" How shall we who **died to sin** live any longer in it? Do you not **know** as many as were baptized into Christ Jesus were baptized into His death? (vv. 1-3).

Therefore we were **buried** with Him through baptism into **death,** that just as Christ was **raised** from the dead by the glory of the Father, even so we **should walk** in newness of life.(v. 5). We should not follow the memories of our **old nature [the flesh]** as if we were still under its evil influence (Study II Corinthians 5:17; Ephesians 4:20-24; Galatians 5:24; Colossians 3:9-10). Give Him praise and glory!

DEAD TO SIN—ALIVE TO CHRIST

Now if we have died with Christ, we believe that we shall also live with Him (v. 8). Paul is not only speaking of our living with Christ throughout eternity, but also that all who have died with Christ, will live a life here, that is fully consistent with His holiness.

Again, Paul is not speaking of an unbeliever trying to save him or herself, but rather a saved believer trying to live right. It is the conflict between his or her old nature and new nature living together in the believer. When most Christians get into trouble, it is the direct result of their trying to manage again through the old man (the flesh). The flesh is unable to save or sanctify, but it will certainly try to be dominate. So our own good intentions accomplish little.

Paul is not speaking here of an unsaved person trying to save Him or herself—but of a saved man or woman trying to live right!

The Conflict of Natures

I spoke earlier of the conflict between the old nature and the new nature; which live together in the believer. In contrast to the old nature which does nothing but sin; the new nature cannot sin. Notice the Scripture says, *"Whoever has been born of God does not sin, for **His seed remains in him;** and he cannot sin, because he [or she] has been born of God.* The genuine believer's habitual lifestyle of righteousness stands in sharp contrast to those who practice a sinful lifestyle. Sin shall **not** have dominion over the Christian, because he or she is not under the law [which cannot save, nor sanctify the believer's walk] *but under grace* (Romans 6:14). Please understand grace does not free us from all requirements, just from the requirements as detailed in the old law of the Old Testament. Now that we serve a new Master, we also are obligated to follow His commands:

*Do you not know that to whom you present yourselves slaves to obey, you are that one's slaves whom you obey, whether of sin leading to death, or of obedience leading to righteousness? I speak in human terms because of the weakness of your flesh. For just as you presented your members as slaves of uncleanness, and of lawlessness leading to more **lawlessness**, so now present your members as slaves of **righteousness** for holiness (vv. 16, 19).*

The person who *mixes* law and grace is teaching that salvation is by grace but you must obey the rules of the Law, is in fact under the Law, and sin *does have dominion over him or her.* That person will soon experience the *strength of sin,* the *defeat of sin,* and discover that the Law is holy and blameless, *but he or she is* <u>carnal</u>, *"sold under sin."*

Any theory of the Christian life, which downplays the seriousness of sin even in the ongoing struggle as in Romans 7, is bound to result in unbiblical and unhealthy schemes of sanctification.

This carnality has embedded itself so effectively in the practical theology of much of the American Church; that it is accepted as a norm. We hear it coined as post-modernism and some even call it post-Christian. These people give grace a nod, turn to their own strength and try their very best to keep the law. As a result, many of our churches are loaded with Christians, who are living fractured and defeated lives far below their potential and Christian witness. To all who read these lines, please embrace the Bible truth that, "salvation is *all* grace [unmerited favor and mercy] minus law!"

- We are *saved* by grace.
- We are *kept* through grace.

We will stand in the presence of Almighty God free from condemnation [the divine guilty verdict] because of the finished work of our Lord and Savior, Jesus Christ and *not* because of any work we have done in this body.

*For what **I** am doing, **I** do not understand. For what **I** will do, that **I** do not practice; but what **I** hate, that **I** do. If then **I** do what **I** will not to do, **I** agree with the law that it is good (Romans 7:15-16).*

In these verses we have two **"I"s.** They are contending one with the other; and they represent the old nature [the flesh] and the new nature [the Spirit] of Paul. It is Saul of Tarsus in conflict with Paul the apostle. They both live in the same body. Many believers are in *spiritual ignorance* concerning the two natures of a Christian. Because of this spiritual ignorance, many believers suffer shipwreck and defeat, hurt, heartaches and pains which they would never experience if they understood the difference between *the inner man* and *the flesh.*

As long as we live in this life,
we will have warfare between the Spirit and the flesh.

It is clear that Paul is recounting his experiences as a *saved* man. He desires to do well and he hates sin. No *unsaved* person does that. The *failure* of Paul to achieve his purpose is found in the fact that he is attempting in his own strength that which can be accomplished only in the supernatural power of the Holy Spirit. Jesus said, *". . . . Without Me you can do nothing" (see John 15:5).* Please notice, hypocrisy which is often mistakenly named in many cases as the cause of the struggle is not the subject here. His state could not be blamed on nor accredited to his wrong attitude toward the holy law of God. He declared it was indwelling sin [the indwelling evil nature] that brought about his failure to live as he *desired* to live.

- He confesses in verse 18 that he desires to do good.
- He wants to do good, and he knows the good he should do;
- He is *powerless* to perform it.
- He was constantly desirous of doing God's will.

This *"will" that was constantly "present with" him* came from his new nature. **". . . partakers of the divine nature, having escaped the corruption that is in the world through lust.** (II Peter 1:4).

Jesus Christ is the "Channel of Deliverance"

"O wretched man that I am! Who will deliver me from this body of death? I thank God through Jesus Christ our Lord! So then, with the mind I myself serve the law of God, but with the flesh the law of sin (vv. 24, 25). So this is the unchanging character of the two principles within me. God's holy law is dear to my **renewed mind (see Romans 12:1, 2),** and has the willing service of my **new man (see II Corinthians 5:17).** Untold numbers of believers suffer many defeats, simply because they have not learned to walk in the Spirit and thereby *refrain from fulfilling the lust of the flesh.* "Christ in you" is "the hope of glory," and Christ reigning in your heart and in your daily practices of life brings victory. We can overcome by faith through embracing the authentic Christ. Note the following biblical truths:

- Greater is He that is within me, than he that is in the world (I John 4:4).
- Whosoever is born of God overcomes the world, but the victory comes only by faith (I John 5:4).
- It is not by keeping the law, or trying to practice the law, that we are victorious over the world, the flesh, and the devil. We can never be victorious except through the power of the Holy Spirit.
- The Spirit of God draws us to God.
- The Holy Spirit is the attending Physician at the new birth.
- We are born of the Spirit.
- He baptizes us into the body of Christ when we accept Jesus by faith.
- He seals us until the day of redemption, and from the moment we are born again until that glad day when we stand in the presence of our Redeemer.
- It is the Holy Spirit of God who leads us in the path of victory over the world, the flesh, and the devil.

The Word of God can't stop you from sinning—but if you are in right relationship with Christ, it will keep you from sinning!—Jay R. Leach.

In Romans 7 we hear the pitiful cry of a believer who is a bond slave "of the flesh," his members bond slaves to sin, but thank God for relief in chapter 8. Here the same believer cries out in victory, **"Who shall separate us from the love of Christ? We are more than conquerors through Him that loved us" (Chapter 8:35, 37).**

STUDY SUMMARY

CHAPTER 11

THE STRUGGLE IN THE CHRISTIAN'S LIFE

How is our relationship in Christ different from an earthly relationship?

II Corinthians 5:17 says, "If anyone is in Christ he is a new creation; old things have passed away, behold, all things have become new."

Is it true that Christ gave the believer His righteousness in salvation?

For He made Him who knew no sin to be sin for us, that we might become the righteousness of God in Him (2 Corinthians 5:21).

How should believers live after receiving justification?

Because it is written, "Be holy, for I am holy" (I Peter 1:16).

How did Paul describe the church at Corinth?

To the church of God which is at Corinth, to those who are _sanctified_ in Christ Jesus, called to be _saints_ with all who in every place call on the name of Jesus our Lord (see 1 Corinthians 1:2).

Does Scripture support the statement, "All believers have been sanctified, but not all believers live sanctified lives?

Many Scripture passages support this position including 1 Peter 2:9-11, **"But you are a chosen generation, a royal priesthood, a holy nation. His own special people, that you may proclaim** the praises of Him who called you out of darkness into the marvelous light; who once were not a people but are now the people of God, who had not obtained mercy but now have obtained. Beloved, I beg you as sojourners and pilgrims <u>abstain from fleshly lusts</u> which war against the soul."

Shall we continue in sin?

Paul shouts, "Certainly not! How shall we who died to sin live any longer in it? Do you not know as many as were baptized into Christ Jesus were baptized into His death?" (see Romans 6:1-3).

Chapter 12

JESUS CHRIST—OUR CHANNEL OF DELIVERANCE

The Bible teaches us what we are because of our spiritual birth and union with Christ. Notice, most of the Epistles begin by stating what God made us because of our position *in Christ*. Because of this exalted position, we are declared to be: **"the righteousness of God"** (2 Corinthians 5:21); **"justified"** (Romans 5:1); **"sanctified"** and **"redeemed"** 1(1 Corinthians 1:30); **"forgiven of all sin"** Colossians 2:13-14; **"made a totally new creation"** (2 Corinthians 5:17; **"partakers of the divine nature"** (2 Peter 1:4); **"have put on the new man"** (Colossians 3:10); **"given an inheritance that cannot be taken away"** (1 Peter 1:4); **"accepted in the Beloved"** (Ephesians 1:6) and the precious promise which I will expand on in this chapter: **"deliverance from all condemnation"** (Romans 8:1).

The Struggle is over

Paul joyfully proclaims his wonderful answer found to his question, *"in Christ Jesus:"* **"Thanks be to God through Jesus Christ our LORD! . . . . There is therefore now no condemnation for those who are in Christ Jesus"** (Romans 7:25a-8:1). Victory over the sin nature begins with our understanding and believing in the perfect, and completed atoning work of our Lord and Savior, Jesus Christ. Jesus Christ has already been condemned for *all* of our sins, so since we are in Christ, we cannot be re-condemned for the sins He has already paid in full. God wants us *to know* that the law of double jeopardy applies here; no one can be tried twice for the same crime. When we really understand this truth, we should shout this verse from the housetops, **"There is therefore now no condemnation** *[refers to a verdict of guilty and the penalty that verdict demands]* **for those who are IN CHRIST JESUS, who do not walk according to the flesh, but according to the Spirit."** (Romans 8:1). Added emphasis throughout is mine.

Right Motivation

The significance of all that we have covered so far, as achieving victory over the flesh is concerned, is that it gives us the right *motivation* for living for the LORD. We don't have to walk in fear of being **condemned** and **disowned** for our sins. Praise God!

Satan loves to get the Christian focused inward on his or her sins and failures. A good old "guilt trip" makes his day for he knows it will paralyze the faith of the most sincere Christian.

Therefore, the only viable motivation for the Christian is living in right relationship with Christ and serving Him out of a loving and grateful heart for all He has already given to us. Some Christians' motivation for serving the Lord tends to be fear, guilt, or obligation, all three triggered by the carnal mind or flesh; which operates through the five senses rather than spiritual revelation. The Bible declares that the carnal mind is actually enmity, [anti or against] God. *"Those who live according to the flesh set their minds* or the soul's components [which include a person's will, thoughts, and emotions] *on the things of the flesh* (see vv. 5-7) [also includes assumptions, values, desires, and purposes]. In reality such believers are living according to the flesh with the result of death [because the mind of the flesh is hostile to God and can never submit to His laws] (see v. 6; James 1:13-15). The alternative is walking according to the Spirit. To be spiritually minded means

overcoming the deadness of the flesh and experiencing life and
peace. This is the resurrection life (see Philippians 3:10). Surveys
and polls of such reputable organizations as the Gallup polls and
Barna Research reflect a great percentage of Christians think living
in the flesh is correct and normal. Actually this is simply unbelief
and rejection of what God has promised He has already *once* and
for all given to us.

The Contrast of two life Principles

Paul gives us the new principle for a victorious life: *"For the
law of the Spirit of life in Christ Jesus has made me free from the
law of sin and death. For what the law could not do in that it was
weak through the flesh, God did by sending His own Son in the
likeness of sinful flesh, on account of sin: He condemned sin in the
flesh, that the righteous requirement of the law might be fulfilled in
us who **do not walk according to the flesh, but according to the
Spirit"** (Romans 8:2-4).

We have been delivered from the principle of law as a way
of living because obedience to it requires us to use our human
abilities. As stated throughout, the law produces only sin and
death. Therefore God had to provide a just precedence upon which
His Spirit could come into our bodies and deal with our sin nature
which produces our sins. He did this: *God sent His own Son in
the likeness of sinful flesh, on account of sin: **He condemned sin
[sinful nature] in the flesh.** (v.3). That is, He *judged* the existence
of our sin nature; therefore the power of that sin nature over us is
broken, and no longer able to block the Spiritual formation of His
righteous character in us. Paul says all this was done **"in order
that the righteous requirement of the law might be fulfilled in
us who do not walk according to the flesh but according to the
Spirit"** (Romans 8:4).

The principle we are now live under works on the basis of
the finished work of Christ that provided a just basis for the **Holy
Spirit to permanently dwell within us and produce life and
righteousness.** He is now free to live permanently in our mortal

bodies even though the sin nature (flesh), with all its lusts is still in us. We no longer have to sin! The Christian still has the ability to sin, *but* he or she *now* has an appetite for holiness. The dynamic is still there, but not the desire for sin. We can now say "no" to its lusts, temptations and habits, and the Holy Spirit backs us up. Praise God!

To do this, we must by faith remain fully dependent upon the Holy Spirit and not our own human strength and abilities. To deal with any thought or action that comes from our sinful nature; as we choose 24/7 to depend upon the Holy Spirit to keep us, He forms a righteous life in us that is above the laws standard and pleasing to God. The Holy Spirit produces in the righteous life the "fruit of the Spirit;" which is one fruit comprised of these virtues recorded in Galatians 5:22-23:

Love—The Greek term is "agape" meaning the love of God respect, devotion, and affection that leads to willing, self sacrificial service, and seeking nothing in return. (John 15:13; Romans 5:8; John 3:16-17).

Joy—is happiness based on unchanging divine promises and kingdom realities. It is the sense of well-being experienced by one who is in right relationship with God. In spite of unrelated circumstances. (also John 16:20-22).

Peace—is the inner calm that results from confidence in one's saving relationship with Christ. Like joy peace is not related to one's circumstances of life. (also John 14:27; Romans 8:28; Philippians 4:6-7, 8).

Longsuffering—refers to the ability to long endure the frailties, offenses, injuries, and provocations inflicted by others and situations (also Ephesians 4:2; Colossians 3:12; 1 Timothy 1:15-16).

Kindness—is tender concern for others reflected in a desire to treat others gently; just as the Lord treats all true Christians. (also Matthew 11:28-29; 19:13-14; 2 Timothy 2:24).

Goodness—is moral and spiritual excellence manifested in active kindness (also Romans 5:7; 6:10; 2 Thessalonians 1:11).

Faithfulness—is the living, divine principle of inward and whole-hearted confidence, assurance, trust, and reliance in God and all that He says. (also Hebrews 10:19-38; 11:1, 6; Romans 4:17; 8:24; Revelation 2:10).

Gentleness—also translated "meekness" is a humble and gentle attitude that is patiently submissive and balanced in tempers and passions and in every offense; while having no desire for revenge or retribution. (Psalm 25:9).

Self control—is the restraining in the indulgence of passions and appetites (also Proverbs 23:1-3; 25:16; 1 Corinthians 9:25-27; Philippians 4:5; 1 Thessalonians 5:6-8; Titus 2:2-3; 11-12; 2 Peter 1:5-6).

The most important fruit produced by the spirit-formation of the Spirit is **love.** This is God's love and cannot be produced by any human efforts. First Corinthians 13 describes this Holy Spirit produced love and a picture of what a Spirit-filled Christian's life should be. God's kind of love also allows us to live a life above what the law demands: *Owe no man anything except to love one another, for he who loves another has fulfilled the law. For the commandments . . . . "You shall love your neighbor as yourself." Love does no harm to a neighbor; therefore love is the fulfillment of the law.* While the other eight fruit are temporal, love is eternal.

Characteristics of Love (agape)

- **It suffers long**—is patient (1 Thessalonians 5:14).
- **It is kind**—gentle especially with those who hurt (Ephesians 4:32).
- **It does not envy**—is not jealous of what others have (Proverbs 23:17).

- **It does not parade itself**—put itself on display (John 3:30).
- **It is not puffed up**—arrogance, or proud (Galatians 6:3).
- **It does not seek its own**—way, or act pushy (1 Corinthians 10:24).
- **It does not act rudely**—mean-spirited, insulting others (Ecclesiastes 5:2).
- **It is not provoked**—or angered (Proverbs 19:11).
- **It thinks no evil**—does not keep score on others (Hebrews 19:17).
- **It rejoices not in iniquity**—takes no pleasure when others fall into sin (Mark 3:5).
- **It rejoices in the truth**—is joyful when righteousness prevails (2 John 4).
- **It bears all things**—handles the burdensome (Galatians 6:2).
- **It believes all things**—trusts in God no matter what (Proverbs 3:5).
- **It hopes all things**—keeps looking up, does not despair (Philippians 3:13).
- **It endures all things**—puts up with everything; does not wear out (Galatians 6:9).
- **It never fails**—the only thing it cannot do is fail (1 Corinthians 16:14).

The one great need for the Christian life is love more love to God and more love to each other. Concerning love we must always remember that overriding every circumstance that touches our lives is God's deep love and compassion for each one of us.

The Spirit-Formed Believer

But you are not in the flesh but in the Spirit,
If indeed the Spirit of God
dwells in you.
Now if anyone does not have

The Spirit of Christ,
He is none of His (Romans 8:9).

Any person who does not have God's Holy Spirit is not one of His. You cannot be saved apart from the Holy Spirit:

- We are born of the Spirit (John 3:5).
- We have God's Spirit within (Romans 8:9).
- We are led by the Spirit (Roman 8:14).
- We are assured by the Spirit (Romans 8:16).
- We are sealed by the Spirit (Ephesians 4:30).
- We are filled by the Spirit (Ephesians 5:18).

As Christians we owe absolutely nothing to the flesh. Our obligation is to the Holy Spirit.

- It was the Spirit who convicted us and showed us our need of the Savior.
- It was the Spirit who imparted saving faith on us.
- It is the Spirit who forms the new nature within us.
- It is the Holy Spirit who daily witnesses within that we are the children of God.

We owe the Spirit a great debt. Christ loved us so much, He died for us; the Spirit loves us so much, He lives in us. Daily He endures our carnality and selfishness; daily He is grieved by our sin; yet He loves us and remains in us as the seal of God and the "down payment" of the blessing waiting for us in eternity. (see 2 Corinthians 1:22).

Spirit-filled and suffering

It is only after we learn this lesson that God can do mighty deeds through us. However, the Holy Spirit does not break our spirits so that we are without a sense of worth or confidence. But God teaches us that we have worth because of whom He has made us *in Christ*. We then come fully to have Christ-confidence instead of self-confidence.

We see our problems and opportunities in the light of God's power to deal with them through us in response to our faith. The Apostle Paul summed up this principle when he said, *"I can do all things through Christ who strengthens me"* (Philippians 4:13). In the original Greek this verse literally says, "I can do all things through Him who keeps pouring the power into me." And God also promises, *"For it is God who is at work in you, both to will and to work for His good pleasure"* (Philippians 2:13).

So God simply transfers our confidence from ourselves to Him. He convinces us that He will work His mighty power and wisdom through us. Our faith then begins to grab hold of promises like this: *"Behold, I am the LORD, the GOD of all flesh. Is there anything too hard for Me?"* (Jeremiah 32:27).

STUDY SUMMARY

CHAPTER 12

JESUS CHRIST—OUR CHANNEL OF DELIVERANCE

What is the answer to Paul's question? Who shall deliver me from this body of death?

I thank God through Jesus Christ our Lord! There is therefore now no condemnation [refers to a verdict of guilty and the penalty that verdict demands] to those who are "in Christ Jesus," who do not walk according to the flesh, but according to the Spirit. (Romans 8:1).

Paul gave the new principle for a victorious life, which says,

For the law of the Spirit of life in Christ Jesus has made me free from the law of sin and death. For what the law could not do in that it was weak through the flesh, God did by sending His own Son in the likeness of sinful flesh, on account of sin: He condemned sin in the flesh, that the righteous requirement of the law might be fulfilled in us who do not walk according to the flesh, but according to the Spirit. (Romans 8:2-4).

The Holy Spirit produces in the [new nature], righteous life the "fruit of the Spirit" which is one fruit:

But the fruit of the Spirit is love, joy, peace, longsuffering, kindness, goodness, faithfulness, gentleness, self-control. Against which there is no law. (Galatians 5:22-23).

The most important fruit produced by the formation of the Spirit is:

And now abide faith, hope, love, these three; but the greatest of these is love. (1 Corinthians 13:13).

SECTION V

The Gospel (Christ)

Chapter 13

THE SERIOUSNESS OF SIN

Each day newspapers and other media outlets worldwide are full of stories concerning terrorists, disgruntled workers, husbands, wives, teens and evil toward total strangers, shooting or maiming innocent victims in public facilities, even churches. In any city U.S.A. armed robberies, home invasions, drive by crimes, greed, cold love, distrust and immorality at all levels of society are on the increase. Sin and evil does not discriminate, nor does it meet strangers. It's totally inclusive and gone wild.

Suggestions immerge from every quarter as to the cause and possible solutions for this gross invasion of evil. Yet, evil in the world is getting bolder and more heinous with each passing day. Beginning with Adam and Eve humanity has sought to use external means to heal internal ills. A few months ago a news alert flashed across the TV screen in reference to a deadly shooting at a school in Connecticut wherein 20 children and 6 adults including the principal were killed. The reporters kept asking over and over, "How could this happen?" Others ask why? Most solutions offered excluded God and His guiding principles.

Jesus responding to this condition in human beings in Matthew 15:19 said, *"For out of the heart proceed evil thoughts, murders, adulteries, fornications, thefts, false witness, blasphemies.* As a person thinks in his heart, so is he [or she]. Thoughts get into the heart [sinful nature] through the eyes, ears, nose, touch, and taste. Our actions are determined by what we take into our hearts and let settle or take root there. David said, *"Your Word have I hid in my heart that I might not sin against you"* (Psalm 119:1). Another in

Psalm 101:3 said, *"I will set nothing wicked before my eyes."* The Apostle Paul admonishes, *"Bring every thought into captivity to the **obedience of Christ"*** (see 2 Corinthians 10:5). We should not hang on to thoughts that do not conform to the life and teachings of Jesus Christ.

On another occasion, in John 15:5 Jesus said, *". . . without Me you can do nothing."* Apart from Christ, a believer cannot accomplish anything of permanent spiritual value. Not abiding in Christ has serious consequences. That is the reason why people must be born again and receive *new* hearts. We must constantly remind ourselves that *true* Christianity *comes* from the heart. Notice:

1. We *believe* from the heart. (Romans 10:9-10).
2. We *love* from the heart. (Matthew 22:27).
3. We *sing* from the heart. (Colossians 3:16).
4. We *obey* from the heart (Romans 6:17).
5. We *give* from the heart. (2 Corinthians 9:7).
6. We *pray* from the heart. (Psalm 51:10, 17).

People have a tendency to blame the devil for the sins listed above in paragraphs 1-3, but Christ blames the wickedness of the heart (sinful nature). Jesus explains in a parable how hard it is for men to break from their traditions [the bondage of rules, man-made laws and religions]. Believe God's simple truth! Holiness, Jesus explains is a matter of what comes out of the heart. This present age will be one of storms in the church as radical change is introduced on every hand. However, we know that as it was with the disciples, the storm is not due to the results of our disobedience to Christ, but to our obedience to Him (see Romans 8:28). If we obey the Word of God; we can personally look for Him to one day come and take us home. The many theologies promoted today have confused so many people including a great percentage of Christians. One sad result has been a relaxation in the seriousness of sin. Justification, sanctification or spirit-formed, holiness, love, forgiveness, grace and mercy [essential terms necessary for correct doctrinal understanding] have been abused; and in many cases redefined or eliminated from the vocabulary of many Christian communities. Therefore, they are led to believe that God winks at sin (meaning here the sinful nature which should have been crucified). Repentance and forgiveness comprise the first step. Our whole lives, desires, motives, and plans must be surrendered to God. Each Christian must die to *self* and completely give your all to Christ. Actually, the total opposite of this Biblical truth is promoted today.

The world promotes self-esteem—the Bible promotes Christ-esteem.

In Romans 12:1-2, the Apostle Paul entreats believers,

"I beseech you therefore,
brethren, by the mercies of God,
that you present your bodies a living sacrifice,
holy,
acceptable to God,
which is your reasonable service.
And do not be conformed
to this world,
but be transformed
by the renewing of your mind,
that you may
prove
what is that good
and acceptable
and perfect will of God.

Today many Christians are being *conformed* or molded by the values and legislated morality of this world; which violate the Word of God, and places those Christians that embrace such ungodly practices at odds with a Holy God. By contrast we should use our bodies to serve and obey God; realizing that the believer should be *transformed*, that is changed by the renewing of the mind. A mind dedicated to this world and its concerns produces a life that is tossed to and fro by the current culture.

Spiritual formation begins in the mind and heart of a truly saved person. A mind dedicated to the truth of God's Word will produce a life that can stand and resist the temptations of our culture by "hiding the Word in our hearts" and "meditating upon it day and night," then the Holy Spirit can guide and shape our thoughts and behaviors. As our Christian life progresses, we should gradually notice that our thought life is being changed from Christlessness, as advocated by the mainstream to Christlikeness. Spiritual-formation does not happen overnight. While our regeneration is instantaneous, our transformation is continuous. We are conformed to Christ's image gradually as we spend quality time in intimate fellowship with Him. Metamorphosis, a Greek term which means to *"turn completely to something else,"* as in the case of a worm entering a cocoon and later emerging a beautiful monarch butterfly.

But we all, with unveiled face, beholding as in a mirror the glory of the Lord, are being transformed into the same image from glory to glory, just as by the Spirit of the Lord (2 Corinthians 3:18).

The Christian is not in bondage by the law and fear; but when our minds are renewed, we can go into the very presence of God and enjoy His grace and glory. We do not have to wait for Christ's return to become like Him; we can grow daily "from glory to glory" (v. 18).

Blinded Minds

Unbelievers have a barrier to overcome because the god of this world has blinded their minds. Through Satan's deceptions today much of what the world thinks to be true is *deadly* wrong! Notice Proverbs 14:12: *There is a way that seems right to man, but its end is the way of death.*"

Too many times when it is too late this deluded person discovers that he or she is on the over-crowded road to **death.** Let me emphasize, it is not that this individual has been tricked, but that he or she relied too heavily on their own "wisdom" rather than turning in repentance to God. The Proverb says the wicked person think they are going the **right** way, but in the end it leads to death! (see also Proverb 16:25).

In my travels, I have come to realize that the kind of message needed today is very fundamental and foundational. Many think that because John the Baptist preached repentance and Jesus came on the scene preaching grace and the kingdom of God, the preaching of repentance is obsolete. So as I stated earlier "grace" is much abused today. In countless churches preachers are aiding Satan's agenda by watering down their message of grace to permissiveness and promiscuity so that it bears little if any resemblance to the doctrine of grace outlined in the Scriptures.

Instead of people hearing that God's kingdom is available to all those who are willing to forsake the world and fully follow Jesus, thousands of sermons are heard every Sunday and Wednesday which presents Jesus as a Savior, but not as LORD. People are told "Jesus will help you no matter the circumstance, or He will forgive you and empower you." However, little importance is placed on repentance, humility, sacrifice and love on the part of the seeker.

The result of this false gospel is so prevalent today and seen in churches full of lukewarm [not so hot] Christians who live self-centered lives and rely on the principles of the world for guidance in life's matters. Jesus told the church in Laodicea, *"I know your works, that you are neither cold nor hot, I will vomit you out of My mouth"* (Revelation 3:15-16). What a shock this must have been to the Laodicean Christians! Like so many in our churches today, they probably thought that Jesus was proud of their programs, by-laws, traditions, and pious acting. Instead of an expected pat on the back, Jesus gave them a stern rebuke exposing their spiritually sick condition in Revelation 3:17-18:

> Because **you say,** *"I am rich, have become wealthy, and*
> *have need of nothing' and do not know that you are*
> *wretched, miserable, poor, blind, and naked.*
> *I counsel you to buy from Me gold refined in the fire,*
> *That you may be rich: and white garments,*
> *That you may be clothed, that the shame of your*
> *nakedness*
> *May be revealed;*
> *And anoint your eyes with eye salve,*
> *That you may see.*

This church believed they were spiritual because its people were well-clothed, when actually it was *spiritually* naked; and [like so many churches today] also believed that physical sight indicated their ability to see spiritually, when it was actually blind to spiritual realities. The church of the Laodiceans as they were greeted in the Scripture means "the rule of the people" like so many churches, a so-called democratic church that **no longer** follows spiritual leadership or the authority of the Word of God. The church is lukewarm, a condition that comes from **mixing** hot and cold [saved and lost]. The tragedy is that this church is **rich** and does not know that it is poor, pathetic, blind and naked. What a picture of the apostate church of today, with all of its prestige, wealth, and political pull, yet all the while spiritually poor. When churches fail to recognize the importance of the Word of God and stops hearing what the Spirit is saying through the Word and starts listening to the voices of the culture, and false teachers, they begin to **turn away** from the truth. We must not turn from the faith (see 2:23), even if it costs us our very lives. We must keep His Word (see 3:8, 10) and not deny His name. Apart from the Word of God, there is **no life or hope** for the church.

Hope for the Laodiceans

When the church of the Laodiceans is mentioned in most sermons or Bible studies there tends to be little sympathy or hope for them! Yet, Jesus did not accept that assessment, demonstrated in His harsh rebuke of tough love. He loved the Laodiceans too much to stand by idly and let them perish in their sin and selfishness. His Message then and today for those in such a condition is,

> *"As many as I love,*
> *I rebuke and chasten.*
> *Therefore*
> *Be zealous and repent* (v. 19).

The devil could care less if you have served the Lord in the past. What makes him frantic and a nervous wreck is if you are living for Jesus Christ _today_, relying on Him and trusting Him right _now_ and willingly obey the leading of the Holy Spirit.

Some of us try to look [outwardly] like we are Christians, even experiencing a certain amount of success in fooling people and even yourself, but just remember, the all-knowing God cannot be fooled. We must submit to Jesus as Lord and King if we are to dwell in His kingdom. Hear the Word:

> *Nevertheless the solid foundation of God stands,*
> *having this seal:*
> *"The Lord knows those who are His,"*
> *and*
> *"Let everyone who names the name*
> *of Christ*
> *depart from iniquity"*
> (2 Timothy 2:19)

Many of our churches are so concerned with what the new convert believes about church membership requirements; that they neglect the importance of genuine repentance. However, repentance *[change your mind and agree with God]* is so essential to the Christian life that it is totally impossible to live victoriously without it. Attempting to live with one foot in the kingdom and one foot in the world in your thinking and practices, is greatly reflected in behaviors such as cohabitation, same sex marriages and unions, riotous living and any other ungodly legislated immorality accepted by many local churches based on main stream cultural thinking over the truth of God's Word.

If you are "young," *seek out* older people who have been drinking deeply from God's love and goodness throughout their life. They have wisdom to share that will help you so that you also might flourish and grow in your faith (see Psalm 92:12-14).

One day we will all stand before the judgment seat of Christ and account for our lives on the earth. Daily the headlines of our nation's newspapers announce the tragic end of the lives of people who where caught up in death without a chance to whisper even a word of repentance. Hear a word from the Lord, *"Truly, these times of ignorance God overlooked, but now commands all men everywhere to **repent**, because He has appointed a day on which He will judge the world in righteousness by the Man whom He has ordained. He has given assurance of this to all by raising Him from the dead"* (Acts 17:30-31).

If we trust the authentic Christ today, He will save us; if we reject <u>Him tomorrow He will judge us!</u>

STUDY SUMMARY

CHAPTER 13

THE SERIOUSNESS OF SIN

Many people are asking how and why so much evil is in the world today; which has resulted in an increase in mass murders, spouse and child abuse, thefts, etc."

Jesus explained in Matthew 15:19 that these heinous crimes and the like precede out of the evil heart, [sinful nature] of people.

Are our actions determined by what we let take root in our hearts?

David said, "Your Word have I hid in my heart that I might not sin against you" (Psalm 119:1).

Can the Christian accomplish anything of spiritual value without Christ?

Jesus said, ". . . . Without Me you can do nothing" (see John 15:5).

Should the world be able to guide and shape the Christian's actions?

In Romans 12:1-2, the Apostle Paul entreats believers, **"I beseech you therefore, brethren, by the mercies of God, that you present your bodies a living sacrifice, holy, acceptable to God, which is your reasonable service. And do not be conformed to this world, but be transformed by the renewing of your mind, that you may prove what is that good and acceptable and perfect will of God.**

Through the god of this world many have been blinded and what they think is truth is false.

Proverbs 14:12 says, **"There is a way that seems right to man, but the end thereof is death."**

What was Jesus' response to the church of the Laodiceans?

His message then and today for those in the condition of these Laodiceans was, **"As many as I love, I rebuke and chasten. Therefore be zealous and repent"** (Revelation 3:19).

Chapter 14

WHERE HE LEADS ME

The LORD is my shepherd; I shall not want.
He makes me to lie down in green pastures;
He leads me beside the still waters,
He restores my soul;
He leads me in the paths of righteousness for His name's
sake.
Yea, though I walk through the valley of the shadow of
death,
I will fear no evil; for you are with me;
Your staff, they comfort me
(Psalm 23).

I heard a minister use the following illustration some time ago: A man traveling through sheep country in the west came to the top of a hill and looking in the valley below, he noticed several shepherds leading their flocks of sheep to a small water hole. The sheep ran to the water and in the process were mixed with the others. The traveler was excited and wondered how the shepherds would be able separate the flocks. To his surprise, after the flocks were watered the three shepherds headed out in different directions. As they began to move out each shepherd began to sing a little song. Each sheep began to follow its shepherd as each recognized its shepherd's voice.

In John 10:3-5, Jesus said, *"To him the doorkeeper opens, and the sheep hear his voice; and he calls his own sheep by name and leads them out. And when he brings out his own sheep, he goes before them; and the sheep follow him, for they know his voice. Yet they will by no means follow a stranger, but will flee from him, for they do not know the voice of strangers."*

Jesus said His sheep hear His voice and He recognizes and calls each one by name. The primary way that God speaks to His sheep is through His Word however, He constantly speaks to us also through our spirits by His Spirit. We need to be alert, listen, and obey the Spirit, and then we'll see God's power and authority in us and operating through us.

There is much abuse of this privilege. However, nothing God says will contradict the Scriptures, nor will He ever add or take away from them. I also believe that the Holy Spirit guides Christ's sheep corporately and individually. We see many examples in the book of Acts. In Luke 2, I like to use the example of Simeon. There was a man in Jerusalem whose name was Simeon **and this man was just and devout, waiting for the Consolation of Israel, the Comforter of Israel, and the Holy Spirit was upon him.** *And it had been **revealed** to him **by** the Holy Spirit that he would not see death before he had seen the Lord's Christ. So he came **by the Spirit** into the temple. And when the parents brought in the Child Jesus, to do for Him according to the custom of the law, he took Him up in his arms and blessed God.*

*"However, when He, the Spirit of truth, has come, He will **guide you** into all truth; for He will not speak on His own authority, but whatever He hears He will **speak;** and He will tell you things to come" (John 16:13).*

*"If you love Me, keep My commandments. And I will pray the Father, and He will give you another Helper, that He may abide with you **forever, the Spirit of truth,** whom the world cannot receive, because it neither sees Him nor knows Him; but you know Him, for He dwells with you **and will be in you"** (John 14:15-17).*

The apostle Paul proclaimed, "And now compelled by the Spirit, I am going to Jerusalem, not knowing what will happen to me there. I only know that in every city the Holy Spirit warns me that prison and hardships are facing me" (Acts 20:22-23).

I don't claim to have any special powers, but on occasions during my years in pastoral ministry, the Spirit spoke to me to lay hands on some people and pray for their healing I obeyed and prayed believing God was going to heal them and He did. On one occasion I had to break the news to an assembled family at Duke Hospital that the doctors had done all they could. [His body was riddled with cancer] they took him home to die. However, we began to pray that God would raise him up for His glory. He did and that father survived almost another decade and when he did pass away it was not due to cancer. I could go on and on sharing God's goodness in healing. The Holy Spirit spoke to me 14 years ago to plant the Bread of Life Ministries; He had planted the ministry in my spirit some years prior. One Sunday morning I started to get out of my car at a church that I was scheduled to minister in the morning service, the Spirit spoke to me [This is the place and the time to begin the Bread of Life Ministries] at that particular church. I was pastor of a church in another area at that time. I shared the vision with the pastor and he was receptive, as the Spirit had also spoken to him. The Bread of Life Ministries which consists today of a Bible Institute with seven campuses and a church fellowship of nine churches [located in five States] was born.

Isaiah prophesied that a day would come when the people of God would be guided by His voice: *"Whether you turn to the right or to the left, your ears will hear a voice behind you saying, "This is the way; walk in it" (Isaiah 30:21).* The Bible is full of other examples and many testimonies are offered daily of God's people hearing and following His voice. To those who are still uneasy concerning the Spirit-formed life, remember listening is an integral part of having a relationship with someone. Consider what kind of marriage it would be if a husband and wife have never heard one another's voice. So it is for a child of God who has a relationship with the Father. I'm sure that you can think of several reasons why many Christians are having problems trying to hear God's voice. Some of the main reasons are:

- They don't take the time to be quit and listen.
- Their lives are busy and filled with things (the cares of this world) that prevent them from getting a quit time for God.
- They don't stop listening to their own soul and mind to hear God's voice.
- They need to stop listening to the news and peoples' opinions.
- They need to stop listening to Satan and entertaining evil thoughts.

Throughout the Scriptures we are encouraged to *"Be still and know that I am God" (Psalm 46:10)*.

For some reason, so many Christians seem to think that God shouts, thinking that He's angry with us. We hear from them after every major catastrophe [God is trying to tell us something!]. Many of us miss His voice because we think we should be able to hear Him over the noise the world is making. We gain much insight about the nature of God and those desiring to hear Him through Elijah's experience with Him on Mount Horeb while he was hiding in a cave:

- First, a great and mighty wind swept through and shattered the rocks before the Lord, but the Lord was not in the wind.
- After the mighty wind came a great earthquake, but the Lord was not in the earthquake.
- After the great earthquake there came a great fire, but the Lord was not in the fire.
- And after the fire came a *small voice [whisper]*. When Elijah heard it, he pulled his cloak over his face and went out and stood at the mouth of the cave. Then a voice said to him, *"What are you doing here, Elijah?"* (see I Kings 19:11-13).

God commanded him to stand on the mountain because He was about to pass by. God has spoken to the world in the giving of His Son Jesus Christ. But He speaks in a whisper, and only those who are willing to get away from the world's noises can hear the Lord speak.

Another very important consideration for every Christian to learn is that God's principles never change, but His methods do change. His actions are never exactly the same in any two situations. David had many victories in battles; but he always inquired of the Lord prior to going out for God's special instructions. Every situation or circumstance [good or bad] we go through as God's children, we should first inquire of the Lord as to what action(s) we should take concerning the what, when, where, and how of the particular strategy for that unique situation. Within every situation we face as Christians we must remember, there is an *embedded seed* of opportunity for victory. In Vietnam our commander often flew above the battlefield in a helicopter for a clearer perspective of what we faced ahead. On the ground because of the manmade and natural obstacles it was impossible to get a true assessment.

Adam and Eve's sin distorted truth to a point where we can not determine it in our own strength. God is the only Source of true [undistorted] truth; it just doesn't make sense to attempt any thing without hearing from Him first for His special direction. He is above any battle you face or will ever face and He worked out His strategy for your victory before the foundation of the world. Oh! What a great God we serve! Magnify Him with all your heart and you'll see those mountains disintegrate. Is anything too hard for your God? We must hear His voice and receive His guidance everyday, study His Word and meditate on it. When we do so, we will be blessed with a number of opportunities that are open for us to glorify Him and share His love through our witness and service to other people.

It's hard for a person with the fear of man to properly hear God's voice; fear negates faith. This person will always be hindered by:

- worrying
- people's opinions
- criticisms
- prevents you
- from moving forward and fulfilling
- all that God has for you to do.

The Bible says, *"Fear of man will prove to be a snare"* (see Proverbs 29:25).

Yet, *"He [or she] who fears the Lord has a secure fortress, and for His children it will be a refuge. The fear of the Lord is a fountain of life, turning a man away from the snares of death" (see Proverbs 14:26-27).*

Herein is pictured our salvation and security in Christ. It's high time for us to throw off the fear of man and fix our gaze on Jesus Christ. We should constantly be reminded of the lesson learned in Romans 6 we are dead [our sin nature] to this world and everything that it represents. Satan and his worldliness have been neutralized or disengaged by the divine nature (see 2 Peter 1:4) to a dead man or woman. All that matters is our personal relationship with God!

A great misconception many Christians are experiencing today is to think that the only place a Christian can hear the Lord's voice is during church services on Sunday mornings. So they set this time [1 or 2 hours] aside for God and spiritual purposes, and the rest of the week is dedicated to the secular. It's a deadly thing to listen to biblical teaching but fail to internalize the message and go out and live what you have been taught. The Bible says such a person is deceived (see James 1:22-25).

This separation unto the secular has produced a culture of Christians who lives by the secular elements as their source of provision and strength. It seems that many of our governmental assistance programs are designed whether intentional or not to create a culture of dependency. In all of my years as a pastor, I've always been amazed that the majority of the people receiving such aid in the areas I served were less prone to even attend church. This separation is totally unbiblical and eats away your spiritual life. God not only want us to get the teaching or preaching, He also expects us to live it out in every area of our lives through the week. God uses and works through people who are willing to obey His Word. Remember it was the *lack of righteousness* that destroyed Sodom and Gomorrah.

STUDY SUMMARY

CHAPTER 14

WHERE HE LEADS ME

How can the shepherd distinguish His sheep from other flocks?

He goes before them: and the sheep follow Him for they know His voice. (see John 10:3-5).

How did Isaiah prophesy that God would guide His people?

"Whether you turn to the right or to the left, your ears will hear a voice behind you saying, "This is the way; walk in it" (Isaiah 30:21).

How does the Holy Spirit deal with the Christian today?

Jesus said, **"And I will pray the Father and He will give you another Helper, that He abide with you forever, the Spirit of truth, whom the world cannot receive, because it neither sees Him nor knows Him; but you know Him, for He dwells with you and will be in you" (John 14:15-16).**

If truth was distorted by Adam's sin; how can we know truth?

God is the Source of truth; therefore we cannot know true truth without God revealing it to us.

How should we handle people's opinions and criticisms?

The Bible says, **"Fear of man will prove to be a snare"** **(Proverbs 29:25).**

Chapter 15

UNITY IN THE CHURCH

One of the gravest mistakes one can make is to think that the words unite and unity are synonymous. Yet, the majority of the friction and dissatisfaction in the Christian Community is caused by individual units [people] striving to unite into oneness. Webster's New Explorer Dictionary defines *unite*—to amalgamate, blend, merge or mix. To join forces in order to act more effectively. *Unity*—is defined as the condition of being or consisting of one. The idea conveyed by whatever we visualize as one thing. In creation the word used for God is Elohim. God said, *"Let us make man,"* denoting plurality or more than one. God is Triune [Father, Son and Holy Spirit]. God is one God in three Persons. God is distinguishable but indivisible. God is one God!

Unity in the Church

The difference in definition between the words unite and unity prevents many local churches from operating at their full potential, thinking that to do so is an impossibility, therefore, they are satisfied operating in a lower state of being able to "just get along." In His High Priestly prayer, Jesus prayed, *"That they all may be one, as You, Father, are in Me, and I in You; that they also may be one in Us, that the world may believe that You sent Me. And the glory which You gave Me I have given them, that they may be one just as We are one: I in them, and You in Me; that they may be made perfect in one, and that the world may know that You have sent Me, and have loved them as You have loved Me"*

(John 17:21-23). Here Jesus was praying for the *unity* [oneness] that takes place through the sanctification [spirit formation] of believers. Sanctification means *"to set apart:"*

1. To be "set apart" unto God, Jesus is praying not only that the disciples should be kept from evil; but they should advance in holiness and service.
2. To be "set apart" unto God, from the world, the flesh, and the devil through being spirit-formed by the Spirit. His disciples are in the world but not of the world.

Jesus' followers had to love one another so that the world may believe in the reality of His love. The greatest witnesses for Jesus Christ are Christians in their loving relationship to one another. The *revelation* of Jesus Christ through Christians *is* the means of unity. This unity can only exist through correct belief and correct thinking about Jesus Christ, God the Father, and the Holy Spirit. However, all is futile if such belief does not bear the *fruit* of [a life that demonstrates God's love and produces the unity between all true Christians]. The mutual indwelling of the Father, Son, and Holy Spirit in the church is the ultimate means for that unity in that it is the ultimate expression of God's love.

Unbelievers recognize true Christians by their love for one another!

Church Unity begins with Revelation

I watched a television commercial recently showing a character gobbling up some type of filth and drainage slime. Its amazing the whole of the character consisted of a face about 99% consumed by a big mouth which covered most of the screen, and a wisp of a body. It reminded me of Satan, the accuser of the brethren, since that's what he is, a big mouth! His most effective weapons are deceptions and illusions *[resort to falsehood, trickery, seeming, avoiding the truth]* based on a lack of knowledge, in this case *[Spiritual knowledge of the Truth]* concerning believers. When Adam sinned and became alienated from God, truth to him became distorted and therefore, except it be revealed to him by God it was impossible for him to know truth that is not distorted by sin. Man [and woman] being made in the image and likeness of God, have within them certain faculties which enables them to receive revelation. However, when man fell so did these faculties. Their mind, reason and understanding became darkened. They fell into a state of spiritual ignorance and darkness.

Gracefully, God has provided the knowledge of truth in His Son, Jesus Christ. So if you are to know truth, you must know God and that's impossible without knowing His Son. Paul declared that the world with all its wisdom could not know God. (1 Corinthians 1:21) and that no man could know the things of God without the Spirit of God *revealing* it to him. (1 Corinthians 2:11-16).

In theology, revelation refers to God unveiling Himself to man [and woman], and communicating truth to their minds which *could not* be discovered in any other way. It is imparted *truth* which could not be discovered with natural reasoning alone. Notice:

"All things have been delivered to Me by My Father, and no one knows the Son except the Father. Nor does anyone know the Father except the Son, and the one to whom the Son wills to reveal Him" (Matthew 11:27).

"Blessed are you, Simon Bar-Jonah, for flesh and blood has not revealed this to you, but My Father who is in heaven" (Matthew 16:17).

"But God has revealed them to us through His Spirit" (1 Corinthians 2:10).

People do not come to faith in Jesus Christ by scrutiny or searching, but by the revelation granted to him or her by the Father of the Son. (see John 6:65).

Revelation is Progressive

The Bible shows that revelation has been given in a progressive manner with each successive portion building on the previous one. Revelation may be viewed in two categories, general and special.

General Revelation—includes that which God has revealed of Himself to all humankind. Creation itself indicates that there is a Creator. The design, beauty, law and order of things, and numerical structure stamped upon all creation points to an intelligent being, above, beyond and greater than all created things. This being is God!

*"In the beginning **GOD** created the heaven and the earth"* *(Genesis 1:1).*
*"The Heavens declare the glory of **GOD**; and the firmament shows **His** handiwork" (Psalm 19:1).* Emphasis is mine.

All humankind is held accountable for their knowledge of the revelation of God in nature. "Because what may be known of God is manifest in them, for God has shown it to them. For since the creation of the world His invisible attributes are clearly seen, being understood by the things that are made, even His eternal power and Godhead, so that they are without excuse . . ." (see Romans 1:19-20).

The Apostle Paul was referring to those "who changed the truth of God into a lie, and worshipped and served the creature more than the Creator" (see Romans 1:25). They corrupted the truth of a creation pointing to God as its Creator and replaced it with a creation that is god in itself.

Special Revelation—General revelation is that which is available to the humanity in all nations on earth. Special revelation is concerned with those acts of God whereby He reveals His power and will to specific persons. With general revelation there remained the need for a more personal revelation of God. This need God has met in Christ. Christ is the sum of all the revelation of God including His will, His nature, His person and His character. To look at the authentic Christ is to look at God; for Christ is the expressed revelation of God in human form.

"In the beginning was the Word, and the Word was with God; and the Word was God" (John 1:1).

"And the Word became flesh and dwelt among us, and we beheld His glory, the glory as of the only begotten of the Father, full of grace and truth" (John 1:14).

When God revealed Himself to Moses, He proclaimed Himself to be *"abounding in goodness and truth" (see Exodus 34:6).* However, as applied to Jesus Christ, this phrase marks Him as the author of *perfect redemption and perfect revelation.*

The purpose of all the revelation of God is that human beings may come to know *[experience]* Him *personally.* People must come to know God in an experiential way. Webster's dictionary defines experience as:

- Observation of or participation in events resulting in or tending toward knowledge.
- Knowledge, practice, or skill derived from observation or participation in events; and the length of such events.
- Something encountered, undergone, or lived through (as by a person or community).

Humankind made in the image and likeness of God has been given the mental and spiritual capacities to receive revelation from their Creator. However, the intellectual and spiritual parts of man's being have to come under the *quickening* and *illuminating* power of the Holy Spirit in *regeneration* in order to be able to receive the revelation of God (see John 3:3; Ephesians 2:1).

"Now we have received, not the spirit of the world, but the Spirit who is from God, that we might know [experience] the things that have been freely given to us by God" (1 Corinthians 2:12). Brackets are mine.

However, I speak wisdom to those who are *mature*. But this wisdom is not from this world or from the rulers of this world, who are losing their power. I speak God's wisdom, which He has kept hidden. And we speak about these things, not with words taught us by human wisdom but with words taught us by the Spirit. And so we explain spiritual truths to spiritual people (see 1 Corinthians 2:6, 13 NCV).

But the natural man [or woman] does not receive the things of the Spirit of God, for they are foolishness to him [or her]; nor can he [or she] know them, because they are spiritually discerned (v. 14).

Bad company ruins good morals

Today many whose names are on the church rolls consider Christianity just another religion; and it's so sad to say many in the leadership of the church also agree with that assessment. Therefore, to them Christianity is external and outward consisting of many codes, rules and traditions. Satan has used this deception in the churches for centuries and in the last sixty years or so has reaped increasing returns.

But because Christianity is not a religion, but a life [in Christ] I don't think we should ever engage in conversations that pursue such conclusions. That "Old Time Religion" of our parents and fore-parents has been redefined and upgraded by the mainstream to incorporate inclusion, the new tolerance, and relativism applied to Christ and absolute truth, along with all the other additives that would make Christianity compatible to world religions. A shining example of true Christianity is demonstrated by the Chic-fil-A Corporation whose stated purpose is: *"To glorify God by being a faithful steward of all that is entrusted to us and to have a positive influence on all who come into contact with Chick-fil-A."*[5]

Because Christianity is not a religion, but a life [in Christ] I don't think we should engage in conversations that pursue any other conclusion.—Jay R. Leach

---

Another positive witness of this Corporation is its being closed on Sundays for church and family. The Christianity displayed here is definitely not the watered-down version of many who give in to the dollar.

I was confronted some time ago by some concerned Christians in reference to their church admitting the unsaved into membership under a "belong and be saved" philosophy of ministry. Their concern was the fact that doctrinal teaching and accountability were lacking in their church; and they feared that over a period of time these [unsaved] people would blend in with their natural talents and abilities and eventually hold leadership and other influential positions.

Church history reveals that this was the practice of many communities in early America where the philosophy of ministry was "keep them around the fire and eventually they will be burned." However, accountability of these individuals was much simpler then. Without a workable pre-evangelism ministry in place, it would be almost impossible to foster such a strategy today. Having said that, it is important to note that church attendance without ties or commitment is on the rise in this country.

I'm sure that Satan has accelerated his agenda through this theology today. I recently read about a group who has omitted the biblical requirement of "being born again" as necessary to get to heaven, fully aware I'm sure, of what Jesus had to say on the matter: *Most assuredly, I say unto you, unless one is born again, he [or she] cannot see the kingdom of God.* (John 3:3). He also stated,

---

"Seek first the kingdom of God and His righteousness, and all these things shall be added to you." (Matthew 6:33).

Old Wineskins and Change

The internet and imagination have replaced some qualifying boards and committees especially those providing ministry and ministerial credentials. As I stated in an earlier section, the denominations now God's [old wineskins] provides organizational models and many other aspects of ministry that could be borrowed and built upon by the post-denominationalists. To just toss them aside as old and not needed would be disastrous for the church. Remember, old wineskins at one point in time were God's new wineskins. God still loves His old wineskins.

In his book, *Changing church,* Dr. Peter Wagner offers the following comments referencing old wineskins, using Jesus' analogy of old and new wineskins. Old wineskins offer a great deal of comfort and security. Jesus said, *"No one having drunk old wine, immediately desires new; for he says, "The old is better"* (Luke 5:39). Therefore, the majority of people will never desire to move into the new wineskins of the post denominational age [Wagner calls it the Second Apostolic Age]. Consequently, they will never join the history makers. Why do they resist? Moving from an old wineskin to a new wineskin seems to be too much of a risk.[6] Of course, those anointed old wineskins who hear what the Spirit is now saying to the churches are excited about change. They will not tolerate the status quo.

Renewal movements of God stand on the shoulders of prior movements. In time of war factories are retooled not destroyed. Tactics, strategies and methodologies are reviewed. Organizational structures must be present and tailored to fit the assigned mission, when people are involved in either the [natural or spiritual realms].

Under the philosophy of "It's my right to do it my way" has neglected and eroded the application of doctrinal standards and biblical truth. Many Ministries are begun by people who are after self exaltation is on the rise. Spiritual formation for many in the local churches is greatly hindered; because many of the old wineskins refuse to move out of the comfort of programs based on science and reason of the modernity days. To do so really denies the Spirit of God from having free reign. As a sent one, I see the need of reestablishing the Spiritual gifts in the church. Even in the small church setting the one size fits-all philosophy ministry all models are not effective. When the Holy Spirit is in the lead the organizational chart will have to be changed. Some positions deleted and others added. We must be careful that what we are assuming as a special calling or ministry assignment isn't simply rebellion stemming from resistance to change coming from some of the old unanointed wineskins.

Radical change is here. I believe we have entered a post-denominational or post-Christian era in our society; which is being fueled by secularism, multiculturalism and the New Age religions. Change is never easy; therefore, the old is better? Take the example of the Old Testament (law) and the New Testament (grace). Which is better? Of course [grace] is better! You ask, why? It's better because God Himself instituted the change. On every hand the winds of change are continually blowing. The church must endure and unlike the secular world, the church must allow the Holy Spirit to lead her through the heights and valleys of these changing times. Sam Walton, the founder of Wal-Mart once said, "You can't just keep doing what works one time, because everything around you is always changing. To succeed you have to stay out in front of change.[7]

- Strategies change.
- Demographics change.
- Ministry structures change.
- Goals and objectives change.
- Existing values change.
- Programs change.

Change is constant. It brings discomfort for a number of reasons. And one major reason so many old wineskin leaders do not want to hear of possible changes is because the changes will pull them out of their comfort zones [in many cases long held positions]. So the new wineskins which I call post-denominationalists are meeting powerful resistance. However, this resistance does not come from the anointed leaders of the old wineskins, but from the unanointed leaders of the old wineskins.

John the Baptist is an excellent example of an anointed old wineskin leader along with possibly Nicodemus. John the Baptist acknowledging that his season had almost passed said things like,

"I indeed baptize you with water unto repentance; but He who is coming after me is mightier than I, whose sandals I am not worthy to bear: He shall baptize you with the Holy Ghost and with fire" (Matthew 3:11).

And again, *"You yourselves bear me witness that I said I am not the Christ but, "I have been sent before Him. He who has the bride is the bridegroom, but the friend of the bridegroom, who stands and hears him, rejoices greatly because of the bridegroom's voice. Therefore this joy of mine is fulfilled. He must increase, but I must decrease"* (John 3:28-30).

Other prominent leaders of the Old Covenant were the Pharisees, and they were definitely unanointed:

- They were the very opposite of John the Baptist.
- Instead of blessing God's new wineskin, they resisted it.

- Since they were powerful enough politically to get their way they tried to wipe out the new wineskin by killing Jesus. I am convinced; Satan was behind the Pharisees attack.

If that is true, then it can be seen as a predictable reaction from some old wineskin leaders toward new wineskins. Paul tells us that Satan will take advantage of us if we remain ignorant of his devices (see 2 Corinthians 2:11).

Let's see if the Book of Daniel can help us to not be biblically illiterate and historically ignorant. Daniel told us that God *"changes the times and seasons"* (see Daniel 2:21). God steadily moves forward, part of His very nature is not to be static but fluid. In other words He is continually providing new wineskins for the new wine that He desires to pour out for His people.

Satan does not like this. His desire is to change God's times and seasons *back* to where they were. In Daniel 7 we meet the forth beast and what does he do? *"He shall speak pompous words against the Most High . . . and shall intend to change times and law and shall wear out the saints of the Most High"* (see v. 25). This "wearing out" of the saints is used in the Bible only in a mental sense. Taken literally, it means that Satan tries to prevent God's new times and seasons from coming by sending his evil demonic spirits to work particularly on the believer's mind. If they are successful, that individual begins to think wrongly about the new wineskins that God desires to develop. They are present in the church meetings assigned to prevent change and to maintain the status quo by using religious devices some of their favorite sayings are, "Wait!" or "We have never done it like that!" That statement is coined as, "the seven last words of a dying church." This religious spirit's subversive work is to preserve the status quo:

- By keeping the individual from moving on to the infilling of the Holy Spirit and freedom in Christ; which ultimately delays fulfillment of God's destiny for their lives.

- By trying to keep the individual from growing in their relationship with God.
- By using religion to keep people from switching their allegiance to Christ.
- By promoting the idea that church attendance or doing religious things brings salvation.

These demons or spirits of religion also move from individuals to groups and continue to try to change God's times and seasons. Here the targets are the power brokers, those who determine the destiny of whole organizations such as conferences, synods, conventions, etc. Satan's strategy is to preserve the status quo by getting people to stick to the traditions of the elders. Today his demons are trying to discourage people from moving into the new wineskin of post-denomination:

- By working on groups, casting spells over the leaders of whole segments of God's people. For an example (see Galatians 3:1).
- By speaking loud, writing on walls, or bringing down fire? No! But it quietly aims for human minds to [wear down the saints mentally].
- By allowing leaders presumably serving God to unconsciously be manipulated mentally by evil spirits.
- By influencing the thoughts of these leaders; since they know they cannot possess them.
- By joining the ranks of the unanointed leaders of the old wineskin.

Paul warns, *"But I fear, lest by any means, as the serpent beguiled Eve through his subtlety, so your minds should be corrupted from the simplicity of Christ"* (2 Corinthians 11:3).

11:3). Jesus tells us, not once but seven times in the Book of Revelation, *"He who has an ear let him [or her] hear what the Spirit is saying to the churches"* (Revelation 2:7).

- Satan's spirit of religion wants to wear us down mentally, so that we do not hear.
- It causes religious leaders to concentrate their efforts not on what the Spirit is saying (present tense), but on what the Spirit said (past tense) in a former season.
- In other words it causes a desire in them to preserve the status quo.
- The sad reality is, "these religious leaders just as the Pharisees before them think they are operating in the will of God!"

Our hope of Glory

In the segment above, several important points show us very clearly the reason so many local churches are being rendered dysfunctional today. The main reason is the fact that the Holy Spirit is hindered from being able to fully operate in His role of the Spirit of Truth. Too many pastors and other leaders hinder or forbid His work. Over the years I've witnessed the ambush of too many good Christian workers who move to the sidelines, totally "worn out" by these religious spirits. Earlier I stated that man's thinking and perspective were distorted as a result of Adam's sin. Therefore, spiritual truth is impossible to know without the indwelling Holy Spirit. Trying to lead a church without hearing what the Spirit is saying to the churches is pathetic and yet so many are trying to do just that. Whether intentional or not, many pastors find themselves caught up in the same religious state of mind that I pointed out earlier [they want to construct their own God and Christ which actually is the anti-Christ]. Paul concludes, *"Professing to be wise, they became fools; and changed the glory of the incorruptible God into an image made like corruptible man, and birds and four-footed animals and creeping things"* (Romans 1:22-23).

Many Christian leaders find themselves caught up in the sinful position of these verses. They rationalize and devise foolish schemes, believing their own philosophies [press] about God, the universe, and themselves. The Scripture said, [they] *"having a form of godliness but denying its power"* (2 Timothy 3:5). "Form" referring to outward shape or appearance, they are concerned with mere external appearances [religion]. Paul said, "They profess to know God, but *in works they deny Him,* being abominable, disobedient, and disqualified for every good work." (Titus 1:16). They can do nothing that pleases God. Some of these false teachers in the church were never saved.[8] No matter how spectacular their "works" all of them eventually fizzle out. Although the false gods which men and women worship do not exist, *demons* more often than not impersonate them. (see 1 Corinthians 10:20; 2 Thessalonians 2:9-11). These unanointed, unbelieving old wineskins [full of the spirit of religion] do great harm to the church [the saints] and the work of the Lord.

What can be done about this? It can be changed! It's time for the church to wake up and get back to Jesus' plan for building His church was, *[Christ in you, the hope of glory].* Paul called this the mystery among the Gentiles (see Colossians 1:27). Jesus assured His disciples that the gates of hell will not overpower her (see Matthew 16:18). It is my prayer that God will renew our passion for contributing to the master plan Jesus is building, "His church without spot or wrinkle." When I was a youth, a common saying among the older grown-ups was, "an idle mind is the devil's workshop." Many churches have become idle and have turned inward and in many cases they are just sitting within the four walls waiting for Jesus Christ to come in the rapture and rescue them from this spiritually eroded world.

However, the Spirit stands ready to refresh those who hear what He is saying today, repent and return to the truths of God's Word. Jesus gave His church a two-fold mandate, the Great Commandments (Matthew 22:37-40) and the Great Commission (Matthew 28:19-20); which if the churches would adhere to will stop idleness dead in its tracks and glorify God by lifting up the authentic Christ, so that He may draw men unto Himself:

The Great Commandments

"You shall love the Lord your God with all your heart,
and with all your soul,
and with all your mind.

This is the first and great commandment.
And the second is like it:

You shall love your neighbor as yourself."

Jesus said, "On these two commandments hang all the Law and the Prophets." (Matthew 22:37-40). These two commandments sum up the entire Law and the Prophets and compress them into the above *two commitments* for the church. Dr. Warren Wiersbe contends the issue is not as some argue, "who is my neighbor?" but to whom can I be a neighbor for the glory of Christ?" It is not a matter of law, but love. While the believer lives under the law of the land, he also lives under a much higher law as a citizen of heaven: the law of love. In fact, love is the fulfillment of the law, because love from the heart enables us to obey what the law demands. A husband does not labor all day because the law tells him to support his family, but because he loves them. Where there is love there will be no murder, dishonesty, stealing, or other kinds of selfishness. It is difficult to love those who reject the Gospel of Christ, and mock your Christian testimony, but this love comes only from the Holy Spirit.[9] "Now *hope* does not disappoint, *"because the love of God has been poured out in our hearts by the Holy Spirit who was given to us."* (Romans 5:5). [Emphasis is mine]. "Love never fails." (1 Corinthians 13:8). Remember love is eternal, Faith and hope will end when we see Jesus; but love will never end. **The love of God** identifies **who we are and whose we are** as we love God and one another; results in yielding our whole being daily to the love and **will of Christ** through righteous living. Through the **power of the Holy Spirit** we are empowered to pour out that [unconditional] love of Christ through meeting the needs of others as we obediently carry out the great commission. This is the essence of what I mean by post-denomination. The new wineskin is the church, the saints who go forth in Christ with fresh anointing making disciples.

During combat in Vietnam I learned the value of knowing how to use a little pouch carried by each soldier in a uniformed location on our web belt called a "first aid" kit or pouch. As a potential first responder, every soldier received prior practical training on the proper methods and techniques of applying the contents of that packet to various types of wounds. If you became aware of a wounded soldier near you, you preceded in the absence of a medic to do what you could to stop the bleeding or whatever needed to be done to save that soldier's life. You would never think of just walking off or simply by-passing the wounded. There was no notice of race, creed, or color as we were all baptized in the same fire of the enemy and drank from the same cup, literally. To us it was camaraderie, but the stakes are so much higher as we battle for souls, for the true saints, its love! Wake up church!

The new wineskin church must be alert to the needs of the wounded and therefore train through one on one, small groups or other methods to insure that each convert is trained and equipped to administer "first aid" by using the pack that our Commander left each of us, the Bible, the Truth of God's Word. The battle of life is raging all around us and there are casualties everywhere who need us. Will you continue to walk on by? The leadership in the new wineskin church knows that equipping [restoring] the saints for the work of ministry, **the spiritual service required of every Christian** (see 1 Corinthians 15:58), for the edifying of the body of Christ, *till we all come to the unity of the faith* (see Ephesians 4:12-13). Oneness and harmony among Christians [unity] in the church are possible only through love and sound doctrine. God wants all Christians to manifest the qualities of His Son, who is the standard for their spiritual formation and perfection.

The Scripture says, "For whom He foreknew, He also predestined to be conformed to the image of His Son that He might be the firstborn among many brethren (see Romans 8:29;

2 Corinthians 3:18; Colossians 1:28-29). This is the goal and continuing spiritual service of the new wineskin church.

The Great Commission

Shortly before Jesus departed this earth for heaven, He gave His disciples the Great Commission which consists of five more commitments for the church: One in each of the gospels and one in the Book of Acts. In Matthew 28:19-20; Mark 16:15; Luke 24:47-49; John 20:21; Acts 1:8. Jesus has commissioned the church [the saints] to go and give the message of salvation to the world [to make disciples]. When combined with the two commitments from the Great Commandments the Scriptural commitments or special marching orders to His church are:

- Love God with all your heart (Matthew 22:37-40).
- Love your neighbor as yourself (Matthew 22:37-40).
- Make Disciples (Matthew 28:19-20).
- Preach the gospel to every creature (Mark 16:15).
- Preach repentance and remission of sins (Luke 24:47-49).
- Be sent by Jesus (John 20:21).
- Be empowered by the Holy Spirit (Acts 1:8).

Make Disciples (Matthew 28:19-20)

The command was to, "make disciples." We are not authorized to modify that order or any of the other commitments above. It is every believer's responsibility to share the Good News everywhere he or she goes. As we go our message to the whole world consists of Christ's coming, His death on the cross, His resurrection, and His promise to return. Certainly we are to take this assignment seriously; for someday each of us will give an account to God concerning how seriously we took this responsibility. Unfortunately the religious spirit has duped many churches into changing the church's priority from ministry to meetings and entertainment. Faithfulness is often measured by church attendance rather than service. I don't know of any more noble cause than bringing people into the family of God. I've often heard evangelists compare in their sermons, "If you had a cure for cancer how you would go everywhere sharing it and millions of lives would be saved as a result. But you already know something greater. You have been given the gospel of eternal life to share.

If there was one person in the world who does not know Jesus Christ, the church's mandate is to save that one. Church growth through making disciples is not optional!

Built into the commitment to "make disciples" are three separate tasks of which all must be accomplished if there is to be a successful disciple-making process. Each of the three elements *going, baptizing, and teaching* share the same prominence:

- **("Going")** Win them! The church exists to communicate God's Word. So as we are "going" we must share the message of salvation. Please notice that is not a suggestion, or something to do when you can insert it into your busy schedule but as you are "going" about you daily life.
- **("Baptizing")** Baptize them! While baptizing has lost much of its excitement over the years; its importance to the church has not diminished, it is essential as ever. This is one of the two ordinances [the other is the Communion] by which the convert identifies in the death and resurrection of Jesus Christ, our Savior. The individual is openly or publicly [to the world] identifying with the body of Christ, after which he or she is received into the precious local fellowship. First we believed now we belong. The Living Bible phrased it this way: *"You are members of God's very own family . . . . . and you belong to God's household with every other Christian."* Christ built us for this!

- **("Teaching")** Teach them to obey! This process is referred to as discipleship. The church exists to edify, by educating God's people. I stated earlier that spiritual ignorance is one of Satan's fatal weapons. This process helps people become more like Christ in their thoughts, feelings, and behavior. It begins at conversion and continues throughout the rest of his or her life. The church is not only called to reach people, but also to teach or disciple them. This *must* follow immediately after someone has made the decision to follow Christ. The church exists to develop people to spiritual maturity. This is God's will for every believer. Church leaders this task is not optional. Paul answers the "why" ". . . . so that the body of Christ may be built up until we all reach *unity in the faith* and in the *knowledge of the Son of God* and become mature, attaining to the measure of the fullness of Christ." (Ephesians 4:12). Our clearest example is the first church at Jerusalem as described in Acts 2:1-47. They *taught* each other, they fellowshipped, they worshipped, they ministered, and they evangelized.

The traits of the early church of Acts 2:1-47 is a shining example of what can and will be if the church welcomes the ministry of the Holy Spirit to operate in their midst. Any church that is not Spirit-led could be classified as an institutional church. The institutional church is an "organized church" which operates on a set of in-house laws. We might find a "dress code," or a time limit for services, "no laughing," order of service that cannot be changed, etc. The Holy Spirit leads individuals and the corporate with such power and mastery that they perform like a symphony. The music came forth harmoniously from the untrained musicians as they were moved extemporaneously by the Holy Spirit. I stated earlier that we must have organization anytime we are dealing with people. However, organization would be much simpler if we would use the same classification that God uses: the people are saved or unsaved. Certainly the leaders and teachers should not only be saved, but also Spirit formed.

Preach the Gospel to every creature (Mark 16:15)

Mark's gospel is very similar to Mathew's gospel however; Jesus added another dimension to the commission. He said to them, *"Go into all the world and preach the gospel to every creature. He who believes and is baptized will be saved, but he who does not believe will be condemned" (Mark 16:15-16).* He contrasted those believers who have been baptized with those who refuse to believe, after hearing the gospel and are condemned.

Paul in 1 Corinthians 1:18 said, "For the message of the cross is *foolishness to those who are perishing,* but to us who are being saved it is the **power of God."** The message of the cross is God's total revelation as the gospel in all its fullness centers on the incarnation and crucifixion of Christ (2:2). The entire divine plan of provision for the redemption of sinners, the theme of all Scripture, is viewed here. Paul's emphasis is not on the act of preaching, but on the content of preaching the message of the cross.

Every person is either in the process of salvation or in the process of destruction. The individual's response to the cross of Christ determines which. To those who reject Christ are in the process of being destroyed (see Ephesians 2:1-2) the gospel is foolishness. To those who are believers it is powerful wisdom. In 1 Corinthians 1:19: For it is written,

"I will destroy the wisdom of the wise,
And bring to nothing the understanding of the prudent."

Wisdom is not merely gaining intellectual skills but the gaining of spiritual discernment based on the wisdom of God as demonstrated in the Cross.

Preach repentance and remission of sin (Luke 24:47-49)

Jesus was considered by His enemies an imposter and a blasphemer. However, after His resurrection people realized that truly Jesus is the Son of God. Many had to change their minds and serve Him. Peter preached this message at Pentecost and thousands of people declared Jesus as their Lord.

Jesus summarized the mission of the disciples as preaching *repentance,* calling people from their own selfish attitudes and agendas to Christ, who died for the *remission of sins.* This preaching would center on God's very gracious offer to all who would believe in His name (see Acts 2:38, 10:43). Jesus made clear that salvation was available for all nations, to Jews and Gentiles alike.

Be sent by Jesus (John 28:21)

The ministry to which Jesus called the disciples required spiritual power. Jesus breathed the Spirit into His disciples. This preparation of the apostles was foundational of the church at Pentecost. At Pentecost the Spirit *unified* the believers into one body and empowered them to testify of Jesus. In 1 Corinthians 12:13-14, Paul emphasizes the unity and diversity in one body. "For by one Spirit we were all baptized into one body whether Jews or Greeks, whether slaves or free, and have all been made to drink into one Spirit. For in fact the body is not one member but many."

Be empowered by the Holy Spirit (Acts 1:8)

The church is not simply a social club were we go to be entertained nor is it just another organization engaged in religious ceremonies and work through natural abilities. The church is a divine organism, the living body of Christ on earth, through which *His* life and *His* power **must** operate. Jesus died for a miserably lost world; He chose to live to bring that world back to the Father working through us.

I stated in an earlier section that every Christian need to move out of the gospels particularly Luke's concerning Christ's birth, death, and resurrection; which is enough for salvation but not for Spirit-empowered service. We must identify ourselves with Him as our ascended Lord on high and yield ourselves to His use.

Christ ministered to the apostles during the forty days He was on earth after His resurrection. Christ instructed them to remain in Jerusalem and wait for the coming of the Spirit, after which they were to begin their ministry right there in Jerusalem. In Acts 1:8, it is abundantly clear that the Lord's service in spreading Christianity could only be accomplished through the Holy Spirit's presence and power in us.

"But you shall receive power when the Holy Spirit has come upon you; and you shall be witnesses to Me in Jerusalem, and in all Judea and Samaria, and to the end of the earth" (Acts 1:8). The disciples' job was [and ours is] to carry Jesus' message throughout the world. Notice the seven different statements Luke used to describe the coming of the Spirit:

- The believers are "baptized with the Holy Spirit" (Acts 1:5; 11:16).
- The Holy Spirit "comes upon" (Acts 1:8; 19:6).
- The believers were all "filled with the Spirit" (Acts 2:4).
- The Holy Spirit is "poured out" (Acts 2:17-18, 33; 10:45).
- The believers "receive the Spirit" (Acts 2:38; 8:15, 17, 19; 10:47; 19:2).
- The Holy Spirit is "given" (Acts 8:18; 11:17).
- The Holy Spirit "falls upon" (Acts 8:16; 10:44; 11:15).

Jesus told His disciples, "Most assuredly, I say to you, he who believes in Me, the works that I do he will do also; and greater works than these he will do, because I go to My Father (John 14:12). How could He say believers could do greater works? Certainly not in our own power, Jesus promised that the Father would send another Helper, who will abide with us forever, the Spirit of truth, whom the world cannot receive, because it neither sees Him nor knows Him,; but you know Him, *for He dwells with you and will be in you* (see John 14:16-17). The Holy Spirit is called the Spirit of truth because He is truth and guides us into all truth (see 1 Corinthians 2:13; 2 Peter 1:21).

If Jesus is Lord! Our consuming passion will be to glorify God by our obedience to His great commandment and His great commission. The current chaotic shift toward postmodernism and the so-called post Christian era with their relativistic ethos, a strong integration of heart and head understanding is essential. And God's Spirit will transform us, empower us, and guide us. "In one Spirit we were all baptized into one body" (1 Corinthians 12:13).

STUDY SUMMARY

CHAPTER 15

UNITY IN THE CHURCH

What was the specific object of Jesus' High Priestly prayer in John 17?

The object of Jesus' prayer was unity: **"That they all may be one, as You, Father, are in Me, and I and You; that they also may be one in Us, that the world may believe that you sent Me" (John 17:21).**

Can the world know the wisdom of God?

No! **"All things have been delivered to Me by My Father, and no one knows the Son accept the Father. Nor does anyone know the Father except the Son, and the one to whom the Son wills to reveal Him" (Matthew 11:27).**

Revelation may be viewed in two categories:

General revelation includes that which Dos has revealed of Himself to all mankind (see Psalm 19:1). Specific revelation is that which is available to specific persons. (see John 1:14).

What is the purpose of all revelation of God?

The purpose of all revelation of God is that human beings may come to know (experience) Him personally.

Jesus said, "On these two commandments hang all the Law and the Prophets."

You shall love the Lord your God with all your heart, and with all your soul, and with all your mind; you shall love your neighbor as yourself (see Mathew 22:37-40).

Why did Jesus tell the apostles to return to Jerusalem and wait?

They were to wait on the empowerment of the Holy Spirit (Luke 24:47-49)

SECTION VI

The Glorified Christ

Chapter 16

GOD'S GRACE

"For by grace you have been saved
through faith,
and that not of yourselves,
it is the gift of God,
not of works,
lest anyone should boast"
(Ephesians 2:8, 9).

Christians have been saved by grace. The grace of God is the source of salvation, while faith is the channel. Salvation never originates in the efforts of people; it always arises out of the loving kindness of God. Truly, "salvation is of the Lord" (Jonah 2:9), therefore salvation is by grace. "And if by grace, then it is not of works" (Romans 11:6). Grace and works are mutually exclusive. Where one exists as the basis of gaining acceptance with God, the other cannot. However, the term grace like so many biblical terms has been distorted and redefined. We hear it used to describe the way a person walks, talks or even how some birds fly [literally]. Many terms used to define the foundational stones of the Christian faith are becoming more distorted with each passing year. This further confuses the real truth of God's Word.

The theological and biblical illiteracy of this generation is without excuse and growing worse as time passes; yet we are the most educationally and technologically prone generation to ever, inhabit this great nation. Having made that observation, what is God's grace? A few of the most familiar definitions are:

- Grace is the unmerited favor of God.
- Grace is God giving us what we don't deserve; mercy is not giving us what we do deserve.
- Grace is God giving us what we cannot earn.

How can you define God's grace? I read an illustration one day about a little boy standing on a sidewalk with his cheeks pushed out holding his breath; a neighbor came by and asked him what he was doing. The little boy replied, "I'm holding my breath because I don't want to use up the atmosphere. When trying to define God's grace we come out about like this little boy trying to save the atmosphere. One thing is sure it is so vast [it will never be used up]. We know that it is nothing we deserve or have earned, and therefore it has to be an unearned gift from God!

It has been my experience that if you try to motivate Christians with messages of fear, shame, obligation, and guilt, the result will be a lot of peeping and hiding as people strive to do in the "flesh" what can only be accomplished only in the Spirit by grace through faith. **But** if you emphasize **grace**, Christians respond with **faith** and depend on the Holy Spirit. As a result, the Holy Spirit is free to produce beautiful works through them. The Scripture promises, *"For it is God who works in you, both to will and to do for His good pleasure"* (Philippians 2:13). I'm emphasizing faith in conjunction with the meaning of grace; because we walk by faith; however, biblical faith is totally impossible apart from grace. In fact, faith gets its very breath of life from the environment of grace. A giant whale cannot survive out of the water in the middle of the desert; so true faith cannot exist without understanding and operating in the sphere of God's grace.

Grace is the means by which we are saved, and faith is the agency through which we receive it as a gift. "For by grace are you saved through faith and that not of yourselves it is the gift of God; not as a result of works, that no one should boast" (Ephesians 2:8-9). This verse tells us that even faith itself is a gift of God to us, so that we should not get the big head [proud] of our faith. Speaking on this very point Paul said, *"Do not think more highly than you ought, but rather think of yourself with sober judgment, in accordance with the measure of faith God has given you"* (Romans 12:3).

"Just as you have once received Christ Jesus the Lord, so keep on walking in Him" (Colossians 2:6 HL). Just as we were once and for all saved *"by grace through faith,"* so we are to walk moment by moment *"by grace through faith."* This is a basic or foundational principle for living the Christian life. We must continue to live by the exact same principle by which we were saved; which God declared is the *only* acceptable way His salvation can be given unto us:

Now to him who works, the wages are not counted as grace but as debt. But to him who does not work but believes on Him who justifies the ungodly, his faith is accounted for righteousness. (Romans 4:4-5).

In this passage of Scripture, the Apostle Paul carries the meaning of grace to another level. He declares that the act of declaring a man [or woman] righteous is apart from any kind of human effort. If salvation was based on one's own efforts, God would owe salvation as a debt, but salvation is always a sovereignly given gift of God's grace to those who believe.

Only those who give up all claims to goodness and acknowledge they are ungodly are candidates for justification [accounted for righteousness].

Good works are important in the life of a Christian, but they are the result of a gracious heart that is overflowing with thanksgiving and love for God. Work done by this motive will receive a reward. But those works done outside of the proper motive will be burned up at the judgment seat of Christ. Paul turns to Psalm 32:1-2 for support. A Psalm of David after his adultery with Bathsheba and his murder of her husband (see 2 Samuel 11):

"Blessed are those whose lawless
deeds are forgiven,
and whose sins are covered;
Blessed is the man to whom the
LORD shall not impute sin."

Enemies of Grace Living

Unfortunately, many Christians today live under the deception that as recipients of God's grace and forgiveness, they are privileged to continue in sin. When confronted they quickly respond that they are living under grace, not law. These individuals actually suffer from a superficial view of God's grace; neither are they aware of the radical changes grace brings into the lives of authentic Christians. Sadly, this terrible deception is active in too many churches and ministries through two deadly extremes:

- Legalism
- No standard of behavior for Christians

Legalism—Legalists lack proper knowledge of the power of our new nature coupled with the Holy Spirit and the Word of God. Like the unanointed old wineskins, they make sure that all of the loop holes in God's Word are closed that might allow Christians to escape their duty to obey.

- They impose and obey the wrong standards for the wrong reasons.
- They constantly add to the Bible's standards of conduct for Christians.
- They insist on additional rules beyond the Bible to make sure that everyone stays in line.
- They keep in place antiquated codes and rules to protect the status quo.
- They religiously keep traditions, customs and special days.

- They impose dress codes, the letter of the Word, and their prejudices.
- They introduce erroneous incentives for obedience to the standards they have manufactured for example:
- Legalism is an attempt to earn salvation by a code of conduct.
- Legalism implies that faith in Christ is necessary, but it's not enough for God's forgiveness.
- Legalism says to gain eternal life you must trust Jesus *plus* join a church, or keep the law, etc.
- Legalism insists that everyone partake of the same standard.
- The legalist assumes that God is going to lead everyone to make the same decision that he or she has made.

Some of the more common rules that legalists advocate:

- Specifying the only authorized version of the English Bible." (Some churches insist that the *King James Version* is the only acceptable translation.)
- "Forbidding certain kinds of entertainment." (That might include movies, all card playing, dancing, raffles and so on.)
- Keeping the Sabbath." (This would mean abstaining from certain activities on Sundays, such as eating out, shopping, or work.)
- Outlawing certain musical instruments." (Some churches ban the use of guitars and drums during worship.)
- "Demanding one method of schooling over another." (This might mean insisting that children be home or private schooled).

We are slaves to whatever controls our lives. In the Bible, both sin and legalism are compared to slavery. Those who try to secure freedom from sin through legalism don't realize that their new master is really that same old spirit of religion we discussed among the unanointed old wineskins in an earlier section. Remember, the new Pharisees in the church today operate just like those of old. Satan dupes some of us into believing that we can buy our way out of our sin through selective disobedience to some moral code.

That's why the apostle Paul compared legalism to slavery (see Galatians 4:21-31). Religious people who are attempting to earn their way to heaven through obedience to God's law are still prisoners to sin. This deception has frozen many of our churches in time. A static church [*operating through human wisdom and power*] can in no way be relevant with today's ever-changing society.

By contrast, Christians who have been set free [through the truth of God's Word and the Spirit] remain obligated to obey the Master's commands; (precepts) which include,

His standards of conduct and behavior for Christians:

1. The golden rule (see Matthew 7:12).
2. The Sermon on the Mount (see Matthew 5-7).
3. The Ten Commandments (see Exodus 20:1-17).

We willingly obey for a different reason. We are now slaves of Jesus Christ:

- Our motivation for obedience is the desire to please Him.
- We have an inherent obligation in gratitude to serve the One who redeemed us.
- We willingly obey His commands (see Luke 17:7-10).
- Our motivation for obedience is couched in His love and favor for us and our love and duty for Him.

Grace gives us a superior incentive for obedience. We no longer have to fear possible eternal separation from God. There is no condemnation for those of us who belong to Christ. (Review Romans 8:1). The world can tell we are Christians by our love (Review 1 Corinthians 13), for God and for one another. Now we can see why Jesus demands:

A new commandment I give to you, "that you love one another, even as I have loved you, that you also love one another" (John 13:34).

You have heard; that it was said to those of old, you shall not commit adultery. But I say to you that, "whoever looks at a woman to lust for her has already committed adultery with her in his heart" (Matthew 5:27-28).

Again you have heard that it was said to those of old, "you shall not swear falsely, but shall perform your oaths to the Lord.' "But I say to you, do not swear at all: neither by heaven, for it is God's throne; nor by the earth, for it is His footstool; nor by Jerusalem, for it is the city of the great King" (Matthew 5:33-35)

We have the right to persuade others to follow the clear teachings for behavior as outlined in Scripture. But in matters (grey areas) about which the Bible is silent, we should ask for God's guidance and allow others to do the same. Any theology in the Christian's life that downplays the seriousness of sin even in the ongoing struggle in that person's life will produces unbiblical and unhealthy sanctification.

STUDY SUMMARY

CHAPTER 16

GOD'S GRACE

Where does salvation originate?

Salvation never originates in the efforts of people; it always arises out of the lovingkindness of God. *"Salvation is of the Lord."* (Jonah 2:9).

The Apostle Paul declares that the act of declaring a man or woman righteous is apart from any kind of human effort, but of God:

Now to him who works the wages are not counted as grace but as debt. But to him who does not work but believes on Him who justifies the ungodly his faith is accounted for righteousness. (Romans 4:4-5).

Legalism is an attempt to earn salvation by a code of conduct. It says to gain eternal life you must trust Christ, plus.

We are slaves to whatever controls our lives. In the Bible both sin and legalism are compared to slavery. (see Galatians 4:21-31).

Grace is defined as unmerited favor of God. It is the means by which we are saved—and faith is the agency through which we receive it as a gift.

For by grace are you saved through faith, and that not of yourselves, it is the gift of God; not as a result of works, that no one should boast." (Ephesians 2:8-9).

Is there a standard of behavior for Christians?

Born again Christians are obligated to obey Christ's commands, but willingly they obey Him by desire couched in our love for Him and others. (see Luke 17:7-10).

Chapter 17

REMEMBER, REPENT, AND RETURN

To the angel of the church of Ephesus write, "These things says He who holds the seven stars in His hand, who walks in the midst of the seven golden lampstands: "I know your works, your labor, your patience, and that you cannot bear those who are evil. And you have tested those who say they are apostles and are not, and have found them liars: and you have persevered and have patience, and have labored for my name's sake and have not become weary. Nevertheless I have this against you, that you have **left your first love. Remember** *therefore from where you have fallen;* **repent** *and do the* **first works**, *or else I will come to you* **quickly and remove your lampstand from its place***—unless* **you repent.** *But this you have, that you hate the deeds of the Nicolaitans, which I also hate.* **He who has an ear, let him hear what the Spirit says to the churches. To him who overcomes I will give to eat from the tree of life, which is in the midst of the Paradise of God"** (Revelation 2:1-7). Emphasis is mine throughout.

The first seven verses of Revelation 2 contain the message to the church of Ephesus, the church at the end of the Apostolic Age, the church that had left its first love. Please notice, the "messages to the seven churches" are located between two visions:

First is the vision of Christ standing in the midst of the "seven lampstands." This vision is in chapter one. The next vision in the book is "the four and twenty elders" round about the throne, and is found in chapter four. In chapter four we see the vision of the glorified Church with the Lord Jesus after the Church has been caught up (*the Rapture*) to meet the Lord in the air (see 1

Thessalonians 4:13-17). It is important for us to note the messages to the seven churches located between:

- The vision of the glorified Christ (Revelation 1:9-18).
- The vision of the glorified Church (Revelation 4:1-4).

The seven churches represent the church age from Pentecost to the Rapture, and when the Rapture takes place the saints will be glorified and given bodies like unto the Lord's glorious body (see 1 John 3:1-3).

The Spirit opens His message to the church at Ephesus with these words, *"To the angel of the church in Ephesus, write."* Notice the same words are repeated in the introduction to each of the seven churches. The message for each church is directed to the members of the local church. I am sure it was the same in that day as it is in the church today. Some of the members were born again members and others were just members. Undoubtedly they had joined the church, but were not born of the Spirit. Paul wrote to the *saints* in Ephesians 1:1. John is writing to the *angel* of the church in Ephesus.

It is easy to pick up on the reason for the more distant form of addressing the church was because the church had sunk so low morally that the Lord could not address it through John as to the saints. No doubt they had declined to a spiritual status whereby they could not be referred to truly as saints; but as babes in Christ, on milk instead of meat. During the days of Paul the church at Ephesus was made up of almost all devout saints; but in John's day the saints *had departed from their first love.*

The Lord Jesus loves to commend His saints when they allow Him to do so. He came that we might have the abundant life, but it is so sad that many of us will not permit God to shower that grace upon us. We settle for less, when it is His desire that we enjoy His very best. God cannot bless us above what we allow by the way we live. Salvation is free and salvation is by grace; but rewards, happiness, and joy come as the result of faithful labor of love in the Lord.

The church at Ephesus was a hard working church. God says, *"I know your works!"* There is no doubt that the good works of this church were many and widely recognized. However, all work is not necessarily acceptable in God's sight. The believers at Ephesus labored and the Lord knew about it. They were patient, and the Lord knew of their patience. They were patient toward the weaker Christians, but this did not cause them to close their eyes toward evil. In this same verse, the messenger declares that the believers at Ephesus had tried them *"which say they are apostles and are not,"* and found them to be liars (also study Romans 5:3; II Corinthians 6:4).

The Lord continued to commend this church, they had suffered much, had been tried many times, but they were cheerful, they did not grumble; they were suffering for Christ's sake. Nevertheless in v. 4, in spite of their hard work, their patience and their hatred for evil, the Lord had something against them. Revealed here is the root of church and individual failure: **"Leaving your first love, Christ!"** The first fruit of the Spirit is love (see Galatians 5:22). In Paul's day the church at Ephesus was known for its *"love unto all the saints."* **But their love began to grow cold.**

The New Testament teaches that *only* what we do because we love Jesus with all our heart, soul and strength will receive a reward at the end of life's journey.

Love is the heart of Christianity! Notice the Spiritual gifts in I Corinthians 12 and the operations of those gifts in chapter 14. The message here is for the church and the individual *"only through love (chapter 13) can the gifts of (chapter 12) become operational"* *(chapter 14)*. The Scripture says, "Without love [agape] I have become sounding brass or a clanging cymbal." (v.1). Many years ago at a yard sale, I came upon a little book I purchased for 25 cents. I have been blessed and used that resource to bless others many times over, through that small investment. It is titled *"The Greatest Thing in the World"* written by Henry Drummond.

In his book, Drummond contrasts what is considered by many to be most important faith, hope, or love. We are accustomed to hearing that faith is the most important element of Christianity. In fact there are many clichés spoken about love in the local churches that tend to lead the less knowledgeable to believe that love is optional. In First Corinthians 13, Paul says, "If I have all faith so that I can remove mountains, and have not love, I am nothing." He then contrasts them, "Now abide faith, hope, and love, these three, but—"The greatest of these is love." Paul then begins contrasting love with other things in those days thought much of:

- Eloquence
- Prophecy
- Mysteries
- Faith
- Charity
- Sacrifice
- Martyrdom

After contrasting love with these things, including Spiritual gifts; he announces that they are all temporal, while love is eternal. Paul then gives us an analysis of the greatest thing love [agape]. Drummond compares Paul's analysis with that of a scientist who takes a beam of light and passes it through a prism [used to dispense light into a spectrum] as it comes out the other side broken up into its component colors red, blue, yellow, violet, orange, and so on, Paul passes love through the prism of his intellect, and it comes out on the other side broken up into its ingredients.

These ingredients which we do not hear preached or taught very much today are vital life-giving virtues necessary and must be practiced corporately and individually to be effective in living the authentic Christlike witness before the world, [as Christians lived in Paul's day]. The spectrum of the supreme thing [love] has nine ingredients:

Patience......................Love suffers long. (1 Thessalonians 5:14).
Kindness....................And is kind. (Ephesians 4:32).
Generosity ....Love does not envy. (Proverbs 23:17).
Humility ....Love does not parade itself, is not puffed up.
.............................(John 3:30).
Courtesy ....Does not behave rudely. (Ecclesiastes 5:2).
Unselfishness ....Does not seek its own. (1 Corinthians 10:24).
Good temper..............Is not provoked. (Proverbs 19:11).
Guilelessness.............Thinks no evil. (Hebrews 10:17).
Sincerity ....Does not rejoice in iniquity. (Mark 3:5).
Rejoices....................In truth. (2 John 4).

These virtues make up the supreme gift, which is the stature of the perfect or [mature] believer. You will notice that all are in relation to people living the Christian life today.[10] Love [agape] never fails!

To know that God is eternal life and God is love. Here is Christ's own definition. Meditate on it, *"This is eternal life, that they might know You, the only true God, and Jesus Christ whom You have sent"* (John 17:3). Love must be eternal. It is what God is. On the last analysis then, love is life! Love never fails, and life never fails so long as there is love. That is why Paul insists that in the nature of things love should be the supreme thing; because it is eternal life. It is a thing that we are living now, not that we get when we die.[11]

Leaving your First Love

By the time the apostle John arrives at the Ephesus Church, the love of the saints was diminishing. The first love of the church means first in point of time and first in importance. The great commandment is to *"love the Lord your God"* (see Matthew 22:37, 38). Leaving the first love means a *great diminishing of the church's initial love,* or *turning away from the love of the Lord.* Too many Christians, churches, and ministries today if honest would admit to this gross sin. The *one* thing that the Lord Jesus had against the church at Ephesus was, "You have left your first love."

When a church leaves its first love it is in a seriously dangerous and deadly situation. Collateral damage can and probably will be far reaching, even rendering the church ineffective for the kingdom in future generations of its existence. Though many churches reaching this state have dissolved as did the church at Ephesus, too many remain busy about many things, but missing the number one priority **[Love for God and others!]**. Jesus cautions every church today, **"He who has an ear, let him hear what the Spirit says to the churches."** (Revelation 2:7a). **Oh God! Help us as a Spiritual Community [Your Church], [Your people] to see and heed [Your promises] in 2 Chronicles 7:14:**

"If My people who are called by My name will humble themselves, and pray and seek My face, and turn from their wicked ways, then I will hear from heaven, and will forgive their sin and heal their land."

Though this message was particularly written to God's people [Israel], the promise is timeless for His people, individually and corporately! It is written in the present tense. The Spirit is promising the church [God's people] today, If you will do three things, God will respond in three ways:

If you,

- Humble yourself (confess) and pray.
- Repent (agree with God and His Word and turn around).
- Return to Me.

I will,

- Hear from heaven.
- Forgive their sin.
- Heal their land.

The nation of Israel [God's people] would become an object lesson to other nations [including the United States of America], who would see the temple lying in ruins and understand the clear message about sin and its cost. God means business! What is the point, Jay? God wants the nations to see that these are and [believers today are also] His very own people and yet, they did not [nor will we] escape His judgment.

God also has a message for today's nations, world wide, *"The wicked shall be turned into hell and all the nations that forget God"* (Psalm 9:17). Passages like this one confirm the New Testament affirmation of a day of final judgment in which the righteousness of God will be displayed and the wickedness of unrepentant humankind will finally receive punishment (see Matthew 25:31-46).

In spite of all the good things about the church in Ephesus, there was a problem. There was a decline in the people's relationship with Jesus because they had stopped loving Him the way they did in the beginning. Jesus asked them to *remember* the relationship they once had with Him, to confess their sin, *repent* and turn from the things of the world and *return* to Him. If they did not, He warned that they would lose their right to exist as a church. They must stop **backsliding** or He will remove their candlestick. They will die out. The choice was theirs. As time went on they continued their backsliding. The Church of Ephesus' period lasted from Pentecost to A.D. 100.

Again, keep in mind that these seven churches represent the period from Pentecost to the Rapture. The physical church of Ephesus has been gone for 2000 years, however, the Ephesians influence overlaps the other churches and we find the church alive and well within the church today. Jesus told the church of Ephesus that they had this in their favor. *You hate the practices of the Nicolaitans, which I also hate."* (see Revelation 2:6).

The Ephesus period was marked by false prophets, and false teachers. Also false doctrines and false practices were introduced by many groups including the Nicolaitans. What they were doing

---

was unacceptable to Christians, and more importantly, it was unacceptable to Christ.

Although this letter was specifically addressed to the church in Ephesus, **the last line is addressed to anyone who will listen!** Jesus has a blessing for **those who overcome** [sin through faith in Jesus Christ]. **"I will give the right to eat from the tree of life, which is in the paradise of God"** (see Revelation 2:7).

In an earlier chapter, we discussed that after Adam and Eve sinned in the Garden of Eden, they were evicted from the Garden. By evicting them God is showing love and mercy toward them, for had they now ate from the tree of life they would have been doomed to live forever, locked in their sinful state. Jesus promises to give overcomers the opportunity to eat from the Tree of Life. It was located in the Garden of Eden, but now is located in paradise of God [in heaven].

Three Steps to Overcoming Sin

Jesus' rebuke to the church in Ephesus is timeless, as we witness the same sin in too many of our churches today. No doubt a lot of churches whose lampstand, the Spirit of Light [the Holy Spirit] has been withdrawn for a number of years. In fact running parallel with the Ephesus age is the church of the Laodiceans of which we read of Christ, the Head of the church on the outside knocking on the door seeking entrance.

*"Therefore be zealous and repent. Behold I stand at the door and knock, if **anyone** hears My voice and opens the door, I will come in to him and dine with him, and he with Me"* (Revelation 3:20).

The context makes clear that Christ was seeking to enter this church that had His name but lacked a single believer. This is literally saying if **one** member would recognize his or her spiritual depletion and repent with saving faith, He would enter the church. This was a people's church, a group who was undecided; who would not take a stand one way or the other *toward Christ or the truth,* and this is the most pathetic, disgusting spirit possible against Christ, God's Word, and God's Church! Christ says nothing good about it at all. He gave them only condemnation. But He does counsel them as to what they should do. What does the church of Laodiceans need?

Jesus counsels, First, the church needs God's gold not theirs (v. 18). Their gold was temporary, its value would depreciate; it could rust. God's gold, His Word, which shows the fact of sin and their need for a Savior, the truth of God's Word was [is] better than gold (see Psalm 19:10-11) and they should follow and apply its teachings.

Second, the church of Laodicea needed His clothing, not theirs. Clothing in Scripture symbolizes the righteousness of God; that only He can give. Their righteousness was like filthy rags (see Isaiah 64;6). When a person accepts Christ as Savior, he or she is given the righteousness of God (see Roman 3:22; 5:17).

Third, they needed His eye salve, not theirs. Instead of having their eyes anointed with the Phrygain eye salve, they needed the eye salve that comes from God. This was a reference to the Holy Spirit who alone can open people's eyes. *They needed to be zealous and repent* (19). *They needed to accept Christ as their Lord and Savior;* He would give then inner peace and satisfaction.

Where is Christ in relation to this church? I repeat, He is on the outside, knocking to get in (v. 20). Christ wants these people, and all people, who do not know Him as Lord and Savior, to open their hearts and lives to Him. When they do, He will come into their hearts and have fellowship with them. Salvation means not only being delivered from the penalty of sin, but also being brought into fellowship with God through Jesus Christ.

As it was given to Adam and Eve after their sinning in the Garden of Eden; God who is sovereign could have executed the death sentence immediately. Instead He had mercy on them and gave them another opportunity. Jesus Christ is the Head of the church. He could have destroyed them all, but through grace and mercy gave them another opportunity to repent and overcome. He promised that the overcomer will reign with Him in His coming kingdom (v. 21). Whether we are approaching or already in the Laodicean age, we are blessed with great opportunities of service. Never has there been such a need for the truth of God's Word. It is therefore imperative for us to study and hear what the Spirit is saying to the churches and share it with others.

We are also living in a time of much spiritual confusion when it is difficult to tell who the real Christians are. Jesus taught a principle in the parable about salt. *"You are the salt of the earth. But if the salt loses its saltiness, how can it be made salty again? It is no longer good for anything . . . .* (see Matthew 5:13). If Christians assimilate something other than the purity of God's Word in our lives, we face great danger of becoming contaminated. Our godly influence and keeping His standards in this world will only happen if we are radically different. We are not identical. We are counter-cultural. We must be separate from the world. The same Spirit of God that lived in Jesus while He was here on earth lives in all Christians who have truly been born again. *"Do you not know that you are the temple of God and that the Spirit of God dwells in you?"* (I Corinthians 3:16). This is a severe warning to any who would try to interfere with or destroy the building of the church on the foundation of Christ. Our Christless society and many of our churches' unspiritual condition today demands that we take a stand. The glory of rightly dividing the Word of truth is that those seeds planted in good ground will bring forth fruit. This is one of the reason why Magdalene and I founded the Bread of Life Ministries, an equipping ministry helping to prepare others to live, teach and preach the gospel in our quest to reach every creature.

STUDY SUMMARY

CHAPTER 17

REMEMBER, REPENT, AND RETURN

What is most important for us to note in the messages to the seven churches in Revelation chapters 1 and 4?

- **The vision of the glorified Christ (Revelation 1:9-18).**
- **The vision of the glorified Church (Revelation 4:1-4).**

What will the saint's bodies be like in heaven?

The saints will be glorified and given bodies like unto the Lord's glorious body (see 1 John 3:1-3).

Paul says in 1 Corinthians 13, "Now abide faith, hope, and love these three, **but the greatest of these is _____?**

Though the church of Ephesus was a hard working church, God says, *"I know your works!"* However, the Lord has a charge against them.

Jesus said, "I have this against you, that you have left your first love." (Revelation 1:4). The first fruit of the Spirit is love (see Galatians 5:22).

The rebuke that Jesus gave to the Ephesus church holds true for each of us overcoming sin today:

- **Remember**—the heights of love from which you have fallen (your first love).
- **Repent**—of your backsliding or falling away.
- **Return or Restore**—your love for Jesus and the good works you did at first.

What did God deny Adam and Eve entrance into the Garden after they had sinned, that will be the reward of the saints in heaven?

Jesus said, "I will give the right to eat from the tree of life, which is in the Paradise of God." (Revelation 2:7).

Chapter 18

THIS IS MY BODY

We've heard that God has a plan for the believer's life, a plan for every one of us. Yet when it comes to our personal call, there is an abundance of misunderstanding, confusion, and disunity. The Book of Ephesians has been called "the Queen of the Epistles." In the military the Infantry [the foot soldiers] was called the "Queen of Battle." I don't know about today's soldiers, but in my day no matter what your specific job description was every soldier was subject to be called upon to fight as a foot soldier. Therefore, we had to go through more advanced training above regular basic training.

Afterward throughout our career we were required to go through specialized survival training. For example, while stationed in Panama as a leader I had to go through Jungle Operations [survival] Training, even though I was assigned to a Logistical Support Unit and not assigned to the Combat Arms. Needless to say the training was invaluable in Vietnam along with the in-country combat survival training there. Continuing education was ongoing until I retired from the Army. I believe the Holy Spirit had Paul to write this book as a technical manual for the church.

Paul's point is that we've been given hope (1:12) and made alive (2:5) in order to grow (2:21) and make a difference in this world by the way we live. "For by grace you have been saved through faith, and that not of yourselves, it is the gift of God. For we are His workmanship, created in Christ Jesus for good works, which God prepared beforehand that we should walk in them" (Ephesians 2:8, 10).

It all begins with a call

As a teenager it was almost impossible for me to pass a post office and not notice that sign out front with Uncle Sam in his Stars and Stripes and his finger pointing straight at you with a "call" to service, "Uncle Sam needs you!" God wants us to understand His "call" upon our lives, but to understand, we must investigate His call. Notice how Paul begins this letter to the Ephesians. He begins with the greatest of all subjects, the call of God. Nothing could be more important to a person than to be called by the sovereign God Himself. Jesus said,

"You did not choose Me, but I chose you and appointed you that you should go and bear fruit, and that your fruit should remain, that whatever you ask in My name He may give you" (John 15:16).

Those who are called and do not go will face a horrible day of accountability. On occasion in seminars or workshops I will ask, "Do you know that what you are is God's will? Do you know that your work or profession pleases God and you are right where He wants you?"

Christ needs disciples. Two thousand years have passed and the world still has not been reached with the glorious Gospel of Jesus Christ, God's own Son. No greater call could exist. The Apostle Paul was called. Paul knew that Christ knew Him personally. He knew Him as his Savior, but also as his Lord and Master. He was not his own to do as he willed; he was Christ's, to do only as Christ willed. He lived for Christ alone! Notice what Jesus said in Matthew 16:24:

"Then said Jesus unto His disciples,
If any man
Will come after Me,
Let him deny himself,
Take up his cross,
And follow Me."

Paul is a very good example for each one of us who are called. Who he was and what he was doing was God's will. His work and places of employment were chosen by God, not him. He had not chosen the ministry because it was a good profession to enter nor because some friends thought he would make a good preacher. He was a minister because God had called him to be a minister. Are we truly called and working and serving where God wants us or where we want to be? Hear what the Spirit is saying!

God's call to the Church and its saints

There is a part of human nature that enjoys things that are sinful; things that are part of the world and run counter to God's standards. As stated in an earlier section, that it is part of our natural makeup that we are born with which manifests itself in:

- The lust of the flesh
- The lust of the eyes
- The pride of life

These three "critters" are the components of a *sinful* nature. Have you noticed they are at the core of entertainment, advertising, and many other things that we involve ourselves with in our daily life in the world? They are also at the core of the natural judgment or selection of a person or thing. This characterized the saint before he or she came to know Christ, before conversion (see Ephesians 2:1-3). Ephesians two is one of the most important chapters in the Bible.

Satan uses these devices in all of his deceptive temptations and booby traps. On one of the cable TV channels, at the bottom of the screen is a constant advertisement of a show called "The Walking Dead," Hollywood has got it going on and don't know it!

Before conversion man lives a life of death. You may be asking, "How can a dead man walk?" The answer lies in the understanding of what death means. Basically **death means separation.** Death never means extinction, annihilation, non-existence, or inactivity.

So death means that a person is separated, either from his or her body or from God or both. A report on the evening news yesterday stated that someone had hacked into a television station's program in the Midwest; and announced that the area was being invaded by walking dead people who were rising out of their graves at a nearby cemetery. While this incident caused some panicky phone calls that is an example of the extent of the natural man or woman's sensatory perception. H. S. Miller says, *"Death is the separation of a person from the purpose or use for which he or she was intended."*[12]

Humans were created to know, fellowship, worship, and serve God, but they do not do it. If he or she worships at all, it is their own ideas and concepts of God, creating a god to suit their own notions, a god that allows him or her to live as they wish. This person does not fulfill the purpose for which he or she was created, having little if anything to do with God. Actually in this state she or he is *separated and dead* to God. Three deaths are spoken of in the Bible:

Physical death—is the separation of a person's spirit and soul from their body. This person ceases to exist on earth and is buried. *"And as it is appointed unto men [and women] once to die, but after this the judgment"* (Hebrews 9:27).

Spiritual death—is the separation of a person from God while he or she is still living and walking upon the earth. This depicts the natural person on earth without Jesus Christ. It's so sad that so many people in our churches are religious people worshipping a god of their own thoughts and notions, yet, rejecting the only true and living God who was revealed by Jesus Christ. The religious person is spiritually separated from God; he or she is dead to God. In 1Timothy 5:6, Paul says, *"But she [or he] who lives in pleasure is dead while they are yet alive."* Brackets are mine. A person who does not have the Spirit of Christ is spirituality dead. *"But you are not in the flesh, but in the Spirit, if so be that the Spirit of God dwell in you. Now if any man [or woman] has not the Spirit of Christ, he is none of His"* (Romans 8:9).

Eternal death—is the separation of man [or woman] from God's presence forever. This is the *second death,* an eternal state of being *dead to God.* It is spiritual death eternally. *"For to be carnally minded is death; but to be spiritually minded is life and peace"* (Romans 8:6). Humans were never created to sin!

The Church Christ's Priority

This is a radical era for Church and State. In his State of the Union address, President Obama spoke of the radical change in climate across this nation and the world through killer tornados, violent earthquakes, tsunamis, and tropical storms as destructive in lives and property as major hurricanes. Of course for a solution he turned to "science and technology." For reasons unknown we continue to look to the disciplines to rescue us from ourselves. God, Christ and the things of God are no longer politically correct to be mentioned in problem solving. While corporate leadership boasts of profits and line their pockets with bonuses, unemployment successes are limited to holiday surges for the most part. Any newscast will convince you that Washington is polarized into the left and right with little or no common ground in between. Over the years we've watched manufacturing jobs moved overseas throwing thousands of Americans out of work across this country. Now our people themselves have become pawns as political institutions and ideologies take priority over the welfare of the people. Many of our law enforcement agencies in some towns and cities across the United States are outgunned by the criminal elements; as a result, some people [for fear] are barricading themselves in their homes in such a manner that in case of an emergency; it is almost escape proof from the inside! The people in any town or city, USA are beginning to face each day with sullen faces, hoping they do not have to make eye contact with strangers in fear of being ripped off if you smile [showing vulnerability?]. The world grows more volatile with each passing day. We are no doubt heading for a political and a cultural meltdown simultaneously! Our prestige as a nation on the world scene is spiraling downward no matter whom among the blue or red win on the ballot. The saying, "If you ignore history you are bound to repeat it" is becoming a reality. Only a senseless person would make the argument that what made the patient sick, should also be prescribed to again make them well. Yet, the political establishment has no hesitation to do so. Many policymakers continue to search out these secular seers for advice. A look back at biblical history reflects that today America and some of the other western nations are mirroring those nations of the time of Isaiah, *"They say to the seers, "Don't see visions, and to the prophets, "Don't give us visions of what is right; speak to us smooth things, prophecy deceits [illusions]"* (see Isaiah 30:10). The only difference today is that this condition applies globally, not to just a couple of countries as was the case in ancient Israel. Some may think that by our advanced knowledge and science, we deserve greater respect: Its shamans always were given respect and credibility, though they were exactly the same, shamans. Every passing year as a nation, we find ourselves turning further and further away from Almighty God and the things of God. God's Word is perfectly clear, *"The wicked shall be turned into hell and all the nations that **forget** God"* (Psalm 9:17). Though I have criticized the establishment, there is hope! Praise God! If all humanity were given over to the Lordship of Jesus Christ, and motivated by true love in everything we do, this country would witness virtuous outcomes. They would demonstrate the full strength of the two Royal Laws:

'Love the Lord your God with all your heart
And with all your soul
And with all your mind.'
This is the first and greatest commandment.
And the second is like it:
'Love your neighbor as yourself.'
All the Law and the Prophets
Hang on these two commandments.
(Matthew 22:37-40).

What is your response? Is there anything the church can do in the face of such complex insoluble problems? Can the church make a difference in this wobbly, dangerous world? Or has the church simply become irrelevant? The need has never been greater for the church to be re-energized and re-dedicated to its *original* purpose, in order for that to take place:

- The church must become the church God intended it to be.
- We must become the kind of "one another" Christians God intended us to be.
- We must learn again to practice deep koinonia [loving fellowship].
- We must learn again to carry one another's burdens.
- We must learn again to share one another's hurts.
- We must learn again to confess to one another.
- We must learn again to encourage one another.
- We must learn again to rejoice with one another.
- We must learn again to celebrate the diversity of our gifts and abilities.
- We must learn again to maintain the unity of the Spirit.

As our nation continues its so-called post-Christian and postmodern journey in this twenty-first century, we *must* embrace the authentic Christ and the true meaning of His Body, the Church of the Living God; which is made up of God's energized and empowered people who live in close, loving, caring community with our Head of the Church, and Savior of the body, Jesus Christ and one another.

The church has been all of the negative things that could be said of her. So I won't elaborate on them as I did in the section above concerning our society. And yet, in spite of all of its flaws, weaknesses, hypocrisies, sins, and excesses, the church has been the most powerful force for good on the face of the earth in every century from the Day of Pentecost up until this present hour. It has continuously been:

- A light in the midst of the greatest darkness.
- Salt to both preserve and make palatable corrupt, unsavory society.

The true church of God will never be comprehended with the natural mind; because it is supernatural. Many even some in the churches' membership think that its primary mission is to be just another social agency caring for the physical needs of people. One thing is sure, if one visualizes the church as an irrelevant failure; undoubtedly such a person is not familiar with the Head and Founder of the Church, Jesus Christ. I think all church leaders need to go back and review the *original* church to insure we are still in the faith.

Many of the great truths of God's Word concerning His church come shrouded in a paradox, a mystery. To the natural man or woman and to the shallow Christian they don't seem logical or at times seems to be a contradiction of God's Word, but when unwrapped, they are truth! Perhaps we need to remember He created and designed the Church [the Body of Christ] to be what He desired it to be. When we were born into this world, for all practical purposes we were children of disobedience and belonged to Satan's domain. However, when we are born again, God translates us from darkness to the light "in Christ."

Two churches

Recently I read of a church that changed their doctrine to exclude the requirement to be "born again" as necessary for church membership. Undoubtedly this church has been greatly influenced by the children of disobedience; Satan's children [see my book *"Drawn Away"*]. I think from what we are seeing in the news it is probably one of the silent issues of a number of local churches drawn away from the truth of God's Word.

True, in fact, that is one of Satan's many deceptions; his real piece of work is the church who claims to being, the only true church. However, if you look a little closer that church is also riddled with sin, salt, and light. How can the church be a dispenser of illumination and grace and at the same time a dispenser of selfishness and disillusionment? In reality what we have according to God's Word is two churches. One is selfish, sinful, spewing hatred, feeding on garbage, power-seekers, persecuting the church, and wearing out the saints. The other has *always* sought to heal human hurts, tear down *all* walls of discrimination, gender, racial and delivering people from sin, guilt, shame, fear, and ignorance through the Word of God and the Holy Spirit.

One is a false church, a counterfeit, parading as Christianity, whose head is Satan. The other is the true church whose Founder is Jesus Christ. This church comprise those who are truly born again, manifesting His true character through acts of love, self-sacrifice, loyalty, commitment, dedication, consecration and truth. Jesus placed an unseen line of demarcation right down through the local church before He returned to heaven, notice:

- The last glimpse the world had of Jesus was on the cross after which the world no longer saw Him in the flesh.
- Jesus came to His disciples and walked with them for forty days after His resurrection.
- Those who saw Him ascend were His true disciples.
- The counterfeit church has no part *"in Him!"* Only those who are in Him are a part of the universal church [the Body of Christ].
- When Christ returns, He's coming for His Bride, the Church without spot or wrinkle. One of the most used Scriptures read during Communion, the Lord's Supper, services is 1 Corinthians 11:28, *"But let a man examine himself, and so let him eat of the bread and drink of the cup."* This passage refers to the way in which a person receives the Lord's Supper. The Corinthians had been violating the spirit and the purpose of the meal, by their behavior; they showed contempt for the Lord and Church. I believe this reflects on the way we do anything for the Lord.

- It behooves all of us to check our attitude and motivation toward the things of God. Untimely death was the punishment some of the Corinthians suffered as a result of failing to properly examine themselves at the Lord's Supper. The wages of sin is still death!

We seem to be extremely surprised every time we have an encounter with the counterfeit church. These encounters have caused some to doubt the very existence of God's *true* Church! But in reality should we be surprised or disillusioned when we are confronted with counterfeit Christianity? Jesus Himself predicted that the false church would come.

GIVE THE DEVIL 1 INCH AND HE'LL BECOME A RULER!—Local Church Bulletin

---

In Matthew 13:24-30, Jesus used the parable of the "wheat and the tares" to describe conditions in the world during the period between His first and second coming; which actually includes this present day in which we live. In the narrative, Jesus said that He Himself as the Son of Man sows the seeds in the field of the world. The wheat, He said represents the Christians whom He calls "the sons of the kingdom." After the wheat is sown, the devil comes in and sows the tares (weeds). The tares is counterfeit wheat; representing the false or counterfeit Christians whom Jesus calls "sons of the evil one." Outwardly, the tares look like real wheat. For a while you can hardly distinguish one from the other, then the heads form and close scrutiny reveals that the tares grows tall but the head does not develop. The full head of the true wheat causes the stem to bend under the load.

Some of the workers noticing the weeds (tares) wanted to dig them up, but the Lord answered, "No! Let the wheat and tares grow together until the harvest, otherwise pulling up the weeds will upset some of the wheat. Jesus said He would send His angels into the field at the harvest to separate them. At that time the weeds will be gathered and burned in judgment and the true wheat will be gathered into His Father's barns. The wheat [genuine Christians] have been "born again" (see John 3:3). In another passage, Peter said, the genuine Christians have been born again not of corruptible seed, but incorruptible through the Word of God which lives and abides forever . . ." (see 1 Peter 1:23). The counterfeit Christians have never been born again by the Spirit through the Word of God. But they make their claim to be Christians because:

- They have joined a local church.
- They have fulfilled certain required outward rituals.
- They are relying on their works and moral conduct.
- They hide their own evil disposition in a outward cloak of righteousness.
- They are talented and enthused.

Again, to the Lord they are children of Satan. The irony of this situation is that to too many Christians, they are indistinguishable from the true Christians. Every now and then some preacher will address the two distinct churches; however, for the most part they are considered as one and the same. Thinking that somehow the tares is a part of the true church has caused much of the division and confusion existing today in the local churches. Another misgiving is the thought by some Christian organizations, denominations, or ministries, that they are the only true church. The point is you can't draw a demarcation line between the true church and counterfeit church; because at times some genuine Christians can, through *ignorance* or *willful disobedience,* display a false and counterfeit Christianity in their lives. When we do:

- We cause as much or probably more harm than non-Christians around us.
- We bring the gospel into disrepute.
- We bring shame and great dishonor to our Lord.
- We can be a Christian yet not live a Christian life.

- We bring shame and hurt to ourselves, scars and hurt upon loved ones, and we grieve the heart of our Lord and Savior, Jesus Christ.

So it is all the more important that we search the Scriptures prayerfully for the *true* nature and functions of *authentic* Christianity.

Biblically speaking counterfeit Christians can *only* display counterfeit Christianity. However, true Christians are capable of displaying *both* true and false Christianity (see Acts 5).[13]

Today the parable of the wheat and the tares is very important for showing in picture form, the two churches according to the Founder and Head of the church, Jesus Christ Himself. The truth will set you free!

What is the Church's Response?

One day I noticed a couple of fire ant mounds in my back yard. I went to Lowe's and purchased some ant killer to get rid of them. I opened the bag and sprinkled some of the contents on the mounds, a couple of days passed, and I noticed the poison had absolutely no affect on the ants. I pulled the bag back out and read the directions; which instructed me to sprinkle the poison then *add water*. I followed the instructions and sure enough it worked! Perhaps that's why the church is confused and has an identity problem. We need to go back and read the directions, the truths of God's Word. Much of our sowing lacks the water of the Word.

For too long the local church has been shaped by the surrounding culture and society at large. We need to go back to the Bible and re-look the directions our Lord of the Church left us. When Jesus instituted the church with the apostles at Pentecost, He issued specific marching orders to His church. It would be to the advantage of every local church to do a check up by reviewing

God's plan, concerning His church! Have we like David with the return of the Ark overlooked a critical part of the instructions? (see 2 Samuel 6:1-14). Other than general revelation, God has never given the culture or secular society insight into His plan. To today's culture the church is a building or an organization. So, true believers whom He has enlightened through the writings of the Apostle Paul and others must let the church be the church without the unspiritual influence of the culture. The young people have a saying, "You know the deal!"

When Jesus told His disciples to *"go and make disciples of all nations"* (see Matthew 28:19) He was delivering as I stated earlier a [command to His people], the church that would shortly be established. The church was given a mission, which was part of His wider plan of redemption and restoration of all things:

- Jesus Christ initiated the first step of His plan when He gave His life as a ransom through death on the cross.
- His second step was to activate His Holy Spirit filled people, [the Church] who would be His agent to spread the kingdom message after Pentecost.
- The Church is the *visible* manifestation of Christ Himself.

Jesus' Church wouldn't be some stationary organization concerned with building an institution or a memorial, but a living organism spreading His transforming message into the hearts of people. With Jesus Himself as the Head [*the only Head*] of His church, the kingdom would multiply and spread reaching people over the whole earth through the power of the Holy Spirit (see Acts 1:8) lived out in the community of His followers.

In the Book of Ephesians, through the Apostle Paul, Christ brings to fruition the full revelation of His great mystery: *"To make all men see what is the fellowship of the mystery, which from the beginning of the ages has been hidden in God who created all things through Jesus Christ"* (Ephesians 3:9). This mystery made known to Paul by *revelation*, was *"hid in God from the beginning."* This mystery refers to the interval of time between the crucifixion of the Lord Jesus, His resurrection, and His glorious appearing in the air to meet and receive His church. In Matthew 16 Jesus prophesied concerning the church. He said to Peter, *"Upon the rock I will build My church . . . ."* (future tense). Jesus did not say, *"Upon this rock I have built,"* or *"am building,"* but ***"I will build"*** (future tense). As I said earlier, the church had its beginning on the Day of Pentecost. Jesus announced the church to the apostles, but He did not reveal its position, relationship, or its privileges and duties to them at that time.

It was through the inspired writings of the Apostle Paul that we know that the church of the living God is not just another local service organization. The church of which Jesus was speaking in Matthew 16 is a **living organism—the body of Christ,** with a heavenly calling and a definite promise. The church will be caught up into the clouds to meet the Lord in the air; and the dead in Christ shall rise first, then those saints that are alive will be changed in the twinkling of an eye (see I Corinthians 15:32; I Thessalonians 4:13-18). Additionally, it was Paul that God used to reveal the unfolding doctrine of the grace of God that we are saved by God's grace through faith, and not through works.

It is through the writings of Paul that our justification, our sanctification or spiritual formation, our victory and finally the glory we will share with Jesus are all ours because of His sacrificial death on the cross, through which He purchased the redemption, righteousness, and glory for every believer. Paul made it clear to all to whom he spoke and wrote that his message was neither of man nor by man; but was a direct revelation from Almighty God through Jesus Christ.

The New Testament uses no less than six pictures to describe the church, please note, none of the pictures are about organizations, institutions, or physical buildings.

1. **The church is the new people of God [a new nation]—** Paul said to the churches at Ephesus, now *"Jews and Gentiles are joined together in His church. This was His plan from all eternity, and it has now been carried out*

through Christ Jesus our Lord" (see Ephesians 3:10-11, 19; Galatians 6:15-16). Jesus commissioned His church as a community of hope for all nations.

2. **The church is God's family**—Paul explained to the Gentiles, "Now you are no longer strangers and foreigners, but fellow citizens with the saints and members of the household of God, having been built on the foundation of the apostles and prophets, Jesus Christ Himself being the chief cornerstone" (Ephesians 2:19-20). As Christians we are adopted into God's family, His church. We become His children, the sons and daughters of God (see Romans 8:14-17).

3. **The church is the body of Christ**—"The church is His body; it is filled by Christ, who fills everything everywhere with His presence" (see Ephesians 2:20-23). *"For as we have many members in one body, but all members do not have the same function, so we being many are one in Christ, and individually members of one another"* (Romans 12:4-5). As the human body is a *unity* with many members each having its own functions, so is the body of Christ. The church is a unified body under the headship of Christ, but the members have different functions (see I Corinthians 12:11, 18, 28).

4. **The church is a holy temple where God lives**—"Those of us who believe," Paul stated, "are carefully joined together, becoming a holy temple for the Lord. Through Him you Gentiles are also joined together as part of this dwelling where God lives by His Spirit" (Ephesians 2:21-22). *"Don't you realize that all of you together are the temple of God and that the Spirit of God lives in you now?"* (see I Corinthians 3:16).

5. **The church is Christ's pure bride**—Paul tells, "Husbands to love their wives, as also Christ loved the church and gave Himself for her, that He might sanctify and cleanse her with the washing of water by the Word, that He might present her to Himself a glorious church, not having spot or

wrinkle or any such thing, but that she should be holy and without blemish" (Ephesians 5:25-27). Paul emphasizes for husbands to love their wives self-sacrificially, as they emulate Christ's love, the kind of love that is willing to lay down one's life for another person and serve that person even if it means suffering.

6. **The church is Christ's agent to fulfill His mission to redeem the lost**—Paul told the church in Corinth and the Christians throughout Greece that, "God has given us *"the ministry of reconciliation." Now then, we are ambassadors for Christ, as though God were pleading through us; we implore you on Christ's behalf, be reconciled to God"* (II Corinthians 5:18, 20). God has given (every believer) the ministry of reconciling people to Him. We may never get the individual into our local church who we meet on our job, in the grocery store lines, or wherever we might meet them, but we must bring them to Jesus Christ! As Christ's ambassadors His message is our first priority.

All believers of every generation who are being called from all across the world are being fitted into God's universal building only by Jesus Christ. A man or woman must build upon the foundation laid by the apostles and prophets, which is the foundation of Christ Himself. Any other cornerstone or any other foundation constructs some other kind of building, not God's building.

"Know ye not that ye are the temple of God, and that the Spirit of God dwelleth in you?" (1 Corinthians 3:16 KJV).

- The gospel of Jesus Christ is open to all people everywhere.
- There is no place for division, prejudices, partiality, and hierarchy in the temple of God.
- If we are going to be used mightily of God, we must become a "unity."

- The Spirit of God dwells within the temple (believers) to form their new nature into Christ likeness and the image of God's will.
- The effectiveness of any local church depends upon how much it allows the Holy Spirit to dwell within and to control its body of members.

"Therefore, my beloved brethren,
Be ye steadfast,
Unmovable,
Always abounding,
In the work of the Lord,
For as much as ye know that
Your labor is not in vain in the Lord"
(1 Corinthians 15:58)

The believer is willing to suffer reproach for Christ. He or she continues to minister even when ridiculed, reviled, mocked, cursed, and persecuted. Why?

- Because God is the living God. The Christian's work and message are based upon the *truth;* what he or she is doing is *truth.* It is all for the living God!

- Because Jesus Christ is the Savior of all men and women. All men and women can be saved, actually delivered from the grip of sin, death, and condemnation. Praise God!

The true man or woman of God must labor, no matter the reproach. He or she must share the glorious news: **People can now be reconciled to God and live forever with Christ, our Redeemer!**

STUDY SUMMARY

CHAPTER 18

THIS IS MY BODY

Could the apostle Paul do his own will after his call into the ministry?

No. Jesus said in Matthew 16:24, "If any man will come after Me, let him deny himself, take up his cross, and follow Me."

Three deaths are spoken of in the Bible:

1. **Physical death**—is the separation of a person's spirit and soul form their body (see Hebrews 9:27).
2. **Spiritual death**—is the separation of a person from God while he or she is still living and walking upon the earth (see Romans 8:9).
3. **Eternal death**—is the separation of man [or woman] from God's presence eternally (see Romans 8:6).

What is God's promise to the wicked and the nations that forget Him?

"The wicked shall be turned into hell and all the nations that forget God (Psalm 9:17).

One of the most used Scriptures read during communion services:

"But let a man [or woman] examine [him/ herself], and so let him [her] eat of the bread and drink of the cup" (I Corinthians 11:28). Brackets are mine.

List six metaphors found in Scripture used as images of the church which Jesus spoke of in Matthew 16.

A living organism

A temple

A building

A family

A bride

A body

Chapter 19

BY MY SPIRIT SAID THE LORD

*"Not by might nor by power, but by My Spirit, says the
Lord of Host" (Zechariah 4:6).*

This is the Word of the LORD to Zerrubabel. The purpose of the
vision was to *encourage* him to complete the temple rebuilding; to
assure him of *divine enablement* for the venture, and the *endless
supply* for the future glory of Messiah's kingdom and temple. The
LORD promises these same blessings to the true church of God "in
Christ."

In order for many of the local churches to accomplish their
[people] mission today would require an adjustment of its present
missions, however, that would require change. Some local churches
considering any "change" as loss will tell you they can't give up
one iota of their tradition for the sake of outreach. As a result, those
churches become more and more irrelevant or out of touch with
a generation in *need* of the transforming power of the Gospel of
Jesus Christ.

The present day situation in our cities and towns indicates
the true church should retain its purpose for ministry, and yet it
must modify or set aside its traditional forms when those forms
no longer serve the purposes of the gospel. The church, therefore,
should remain sensitive to the directions of cultural and social
changes concerning the people of the community it serves. At the
same time remain faithful to the Pauline image of the church as the
body of Christ and its great commission concerning the gospel of
Christ.[14]

Ray Bakke cautions that churches must learn to recognize their own cross-cultural missions within their surroundings. In other words, the church must open up and compassionately embrace the diversity that increasingly make up communities including but not limited to gang violence, poverty, homelessness, ethnic differences, cultural differences, and unemployment.[15]

Churches, especially traditional churches that find themselves amidst the struggle, must do the following:

1. Overcome the fear of change.
2. Pastors must orient their congregations to the image of the church as part of the body of Christ.
3. Pastors must teach the church a mission that is consistent with the authentic Jesus in Luke 4:4.
4. Pastors must adjust their ministry focus to lead the charge of community transformation.
5. Churches must examine their church structures and eliminate components that are no longer useful.
6. Churches must place a higher priority on *empowering* people holistically, and building elaborate structures should be a means of supporting holistic ministry [the person's whole situation].[16]

In the Gospels, Jesus advances His movement through *edifying* people, responding to their physical, spiritual, and emotional *needs* rather than through building buildings. In the Gospels no person experiences a Jesus unwilling to respond to their needs. Churches can do this effectively if they take seriously each person within the community beyond themselves. However, to impact broken people's lives, churches must redirect their focus. Instead of preaching for church membership and monetary programs, preachers must preach to the converting of *souls* and to the *liberating* of lives from oppressive ideals and prisons of their minds and society's stubborn, dismal injustice, all of which is antithetical to the intrinsic message of the gospel. Twenty-First Century ministry must move its focus from building churches, and in the words of John Perkins, *"They must take the gospel to the streets."*[17]

By My Spirit

In spite of the shortcomings, the Holy Spirit moves and *empowers us* to overcome. In 1906 The Azusa Street revival found its humble beginnings out of an abandoned church in the city of Los Angeles. It was the beginning of what was destined to become the worldwide Pentecostal movement that focused on the work of the Holy Spirit. It was led by an African American Holiness minister, William J. Seymour, and had particular emphasis on:

- healing of the sick,
- speaking in other tongues,
- prayer,
- *new* expressions of worship.[18]

It is the teaching moments such as these that are expressions in *history* that must be received as being relevant to us today:

- they demand to be taught and
- learned from as beacons of *hope,*
- in our local churches
- reminding us of our rich heritage
- and those Christians "in Christ"
- who carried the cross before us
- with the express purpose of passing it on
- to the next generation.

As all previous generations have experienced, this passing on task must consist of Spirit led actions of the church. In recognition of the younger generation, the older generation [*through the work of the Spirit*] must respond by communicating the essence of the Holy Spirit's *ongoing* work in light of and sensitivity to the *vernacular, cultural, and different theological practices of the former.*

It is crucial that both the young and the older generations understand their mutual allegiance to the missional call of the gospel.[19]

It is the Holy Spirit who takes what is not empowered and empowers it, changing by His power and presence what is weak to strength, breathing life into all that they might live missionally. The church can claim to be *one body,* made whole, resting on the invisible work of the Spirit. Matthew tells us to "Go into all the world" to all nations (see Matthew 28:19). Mission is that which liberates all of humanity from current bounds of sin and death and it is also found reflected in all acts of love.

It is the Holy Spirit's work in the body of Christ as well as in the individual Christian that validates our claims about that on going work. The Azusa Street *revival* became the inaugural moment of what has become the fasting growing Christian movement in history. And it further validates the attempt to *intergenerational* dialogue. It is imperative that intergenerational dialogue bring to pass physical acts of mission within the next generation that is the on going work of the Spirit.[20] The presence of the Holy Spirit, the presence of Christ, is the *common denominator* that makes both the young and old generation a part of the same body, Both believe in the ongoing work of the Spirit, and both are a part of the ongoing work; and *in that they find unity.*

It is by the Spirit that both the young and the old of today are united with each other and brought into God's salvation history, starting with Christ's life and those who faithfully walked before Him in preparation for His coming, to the future new creation of all things. All parts of the church are made a part of the activity of God and His work in creation. We must allow the Holy Spirit to do all of His work through us, one day at a time. When we allow that work of God in our lives, the *power* slowly grows from its infancy levels to the "dunamus" or "dynamite" kind of power the early church knew. Through day to day decisions to obey God, overtime you will see the *fruit of the spirit* in your life (see Galatians 5:22-23). When you grow in the Holy Spirit, when your life bears the fruit of the Spirit, people see less of you and more of Christ. It is through the fruit of the Spirit in you that the Spirit draws people to Christ. Remember, the first fruit of the Spirit is love. God is love!

STUDY SUMMARY

CHAPTER 19

BY MY SPIRIT SAID THE LORD

In order for many of the local churches to accomplish their mission today would require?

The churches would have to adjust their present mission; which requires "change."

Several things the traditional church must do to overcome the struggles of "change."

1. Overcome the fear of change.
2. Pastors must orient their congregations to the Image of the church as part of the body of Christ.
3. The churches must examine their church structures and eliminate components that are no longer useful.

The Azusa Street revival found its humble beginnings in Los Angeles in 1906. It was led by an African American Holiness minister, William J. Seymour. It became the worldwide Pentecostal Movement with particular emphasis on:

1. Healing of the sick
2. Speaking in tongues
3. Prayer
4. New expressions of worship

The presence of the Holy Spirit is essential for proper intergenerational dialogue

The Holy Spirit is the common denominator that makes both young and old generations a part of the same body.

Chapter 20

IT'S A DIFFERENT WORLD (VIEW)

There was a time not long ago when church leaders tried to minister to people as one single mass group. That type of ministry is not the appropriate approach today; because church leaders now realize that ministry must take place among a diversity of groups, and sub-groups by generation. Generational research and studies are growing stronger as the world moves deeper into the twenty-first century. Why is the study of generations important to church leaders? The purpose is for greater understanding of us [humans]. Changes in people dynamics are happening so fast and different since 9/11; until it would be fair to say it's a different world (view). Historically, four generations often exist together, interlaced in a particular moment of time: young, adult, mature, and senior.[21]

A turning point

America is at a turning point in its history. Recent decisions and many proposed for the near future regarding who we are, and the values we stand for will seal the moral and spiritual fate of this nation. The decadence and darkness in America are more profound today than at any time since its founding. The only power that can cleanse and restore this nation is the mighty power of Christ Jesus. The biblical way in which that power is to be manifested is through Christians serving God and humanity *as the authentic church* that is, by being the true manifestation of the authentic Christ.

In other words, the core attributes of our society *language, customs, traditions, dress styles, dominant leisure, relational emphasis, values, and the like* are being redefined and reconfigured at a more rapid pace. In my day the debatable age of accountability was 12 years old; today we probably should consider five years of age. Research has shown that many of life's thoughts and habits are set by five years of age. Most churches in America are holding fast to goals and programs established several generations ago. When there are changes many of them are mostly cosmetic with little or no positive outcome toward enhancing the true mission of the church. Therefore, for the most part those churches can become irrelevant to the needs of all but a very few remaining senior members. Young people have grown up under the tutelage of video games, MTV, computers, videos, internet and other emerging media. George Barna's research concludes that the results are:

- *A new mode of thinking* in which linear reasoning [resembling a line, long and narrow] has been replaced with *mosaic thinking*, which integrates information and decision making [in entirely unique ways].
- Attention spans have changed for the average teenager it is estimated at 6 to 8 minutes.
- The forms of technology used in many cases in our churches are a couple of generations old.
- The average sermon lasts thirty one minutes and is based upon linear arguments.[22]

I do believe the American church is going through a time of testing and transition. It is high time that she assess her current status as salt and light in the cities and towns. The results of such searching must be filtered through the eternal truths of God's Word. Acknowledging the results, we must prove that we are what we claim to be. Unless we move quickly, we will fail our awesome calling to influence the world for Christ. With every passing day the moral and spiritual demise of our culture, signals that to maintain that position without becoming influenced herself has become a significant challenge. And the sad truth of the matter is many of our Christian communities are not properly equipped to meet such a challenge. We have no time to waste!

There is hope

Our situation is not lost, but it is certainly urgent. Godly leadership along with Spirit-formed saints both dedicated to the fulfillment of God's vision for the church is the *only* viable order for the day. Some day God will ask you for an account of how you used the gifts and resources He put into your hands for His purposes. Use this book as a tool to become more effective as a change agent for the glory of God. The only true purpose for living is to know, love, and serve God with all your heart, mind, soul, and strength (see Deuteronomy 6:5 and Matthew 22:37).

While the various generations seem to be speaking different languages; will we stop trying to do the impossible? It is obvious that we must be endowed with wisdom from the Father and enabled by the Holy Spirit in order to understand generational challenges that impact the church. Many local churches simply ignore their young people and seniors, problem solved? No! The concept of generations has been a part of the human experience for thousands of years. The Bible uses generation and generations 201 times. There are references or lists of entire families such as found in Genesis 5. "This is the book of the generations of Adam." (v.1). There are references to punishment being served on people to the fourth generation (see Exodus 20:5). And Christ references a generational triad when speaking on the resurrection in Matthew 22:32. "I AM THE GOD OF ABRAHAM, AND THE GOD OF ISAAC, AND THE GOD OF JACOB." References are made to an evil generation (see Deuteronomy 1:35) and a righteousness generation (Psalm 14:5). Additionally it is implied that individuals have responsibility:

- To *serve* their own generation. Listen to Paul referring to David's *service* to his own generation in Acts 13:36: *"For*

*David, **after he had served the purpose of God in his own generation, fell asleep.***"

- To teach the next generations (see Psalm 48:13).
- To communicate the good news to all generations. (see Psalm 145:4) confirms, "One generation shall praise Thy works to another and shall declare Thy mighty acts."[23]

McIntosh goes on to say, Scripture obviously takes the theme of generations seriously. It affirms the *different natures* of generations, particularly that:

- Some generations are passive.
- Some generations are more responsive to the gospel than others.
- The Bible affirms that there is a natural succession of generations: *"A generation goes and a generation comes, but the earth remains forever"* (see Eccles. 1:4).

It is my hope that you will be enabled to identify how understanding the general characteristics of multiple generational groups will assist you in reaching out to a variety of groups in your church. We can grasp the key to successful ministry in our local churches by observing the example of Jesus with His disciples. Jesus gave a new commandment, *"A new commandment I give to you, that you love one another; as I have loved you, that you also love one another. By this all will know that you are My disciples, if you have love for one another"* (see John 13:34-35).

Unbelievers recognize Jesus' disciples [believers] not by their doctrinal distinctions, nor by their love for the lost, but they recognize His disciples by their deeds of love for one another. To summarize, if we move forward Spirit-formed, with wisdom from God, and love for one another, we will be equipped to consider planning generational ministry. Studying American society today, McIntosh suggests that there are groups of people with shared characteristics and similar interests fitting most people into four groups. Those who range in ages:

1. From late fifties and up are called the Builders.
2. From late thirties to mid fifties are called the Boomers.
3. From the twenties to the mid thirties are called the Busters.
4. Those younger than twenty are called Bridgers [called Mosaics by some].

As a generation moves through time, it causes a generational wave or change. Many members of a group will move through childhood, young adulthood, midlife, and retirement as a group, although the youngest and oldest members of the group will experience these phases at different times. As the group moves along, it creates *changes* or *waves* that are identified *specifically* with that generation. The larger the generation, the larger the wave or change it creates.[24]

Anyone observing our culture today can easily see dramatic changes have been taking place, signaling that the influence of the *senior* generations is waning as the *younger* generations' influence is increasing, and the church is no exception.

Contemporary Reality

Consider the mounting critical concerns that we can list in coming to a truly comprehensive picture of contemporary reality: leadership, relationships, crime, responsibility, business ethics, same sex agenda, gender-based inquiries, racism, public health, globalism, multiculturalism, household finances, and much more.

It is clear and the line is drawn, to influence the nation with the truths of God's Word; and it is imperative that we be *vigilant in tracking the forces of change.*

Before we can strategically shape or adapt to the challenges before us; we must be aware of and sensitive to the transitions in reality. Only then can we devise and implement responses that position us to have influence for the glory of God!

To be effective, we must strive to aim our efforts to contextualizing what we are offering to others so they can see our offering as relevant, beneficial, and accessible. This concept is based on Paul's comments in 1 Corinthians 9:19-23. The principle states that we are to take the truths and principles of our faith and *without compromising* those truths or principles *develop ways* of making them sensible and significant to our focused audience.

The ministries of Jesus and Paul serve as our examples because they were based on this principle. Each time they encountered someone they would strive to understand the person's need and their key cultural realities (for example, language, socioeconomic background, religious orientation, etc.); and *then* respond in a manner appropriate to the person. Given people's underlying assumption that religious faith exists for the personal benefit of the individual, it is only natural for them to assume that defining, organizing, and practicing spirituality in ways that satisfy their personal needs is completely legitimate.

The differences between Christianity and religions are so profound that I feel Christianity cannot be truthfully classified with or as a religion. In reality Christianity is life "in Christ" and Christ "in you;" which is accomplished through the new birth (see John 3:3). One of the chief concerns facing the Christian Church today is to persuade people that the *blending* of disparate religious beliefs and practices into a customized impure version of Christianity is *illegitimate.*

The Way We Were

Church history reflects that for centuries, Christians have been formulating and presenting serious interpretations of reality that were applied to *every* aspect of life and culture. This nation's oldest and highest educational and cultural institutions' founding documents reflect that they were shaped to include their social and moral consensus by the Christian worldview. However, a serious *shift* began in the latter part of the eighteenth century, the effects of which continue to this day. The Enlightenment which sought to elevate man and eliminate God, aided by a growing anti-intellectual spirit began to dominate the American church and Christians. Thus, providing the springboard needed by satanic secularism to stifle Christian influence on the culture. As a result the churches have within the past 100 years become increasingly influenced and conformed by the culture.

It has been the unique influence of Christianity that has produced the greatness of so-called Western civilization. However, we are not to confuse Christianity and Western civilization, or being a Christian with being an American, as these are by no means synonymous. Christianity stands on its own, and where Christianity flourishes it naturally brings with it personal, social, and cultural transformation. Conversely, where Christianity fails to flourish or, more specifically, where the followers of Christ fail to think and act faithfully, cultures will likewise decline or fall short of their potential. This point was reinforced when a leading scholar from the Chinese Academy of Social Sciences, speaking to a group of westerners in 2002, said,

One of the things we were asked to look into was what accounted for the success, in fact, the pre-eminence of the West all over the world. We studied everything we could from the historical, political, economics, and cultural perspective. At first, we thought it was because you had more powerful guns then we had. Then we thought it was because you had the best political system. Next we focused on your economic system. But in the past twenty years, we have realized that the heart of your culture is your religion: Christianity. That is why the West has been so powerful. The Christian moral foundation of social and cultural life was what made possible the emergence of capitalism and then the successful transition to democratic politics. We don't have any doubt about this. [25]

The Chinese scholar had it right. However, these successes are inevitable for any civilization that builds and maintains it's society and foundations upon the *truths of God's Word* and rightfully acknowledge Almighty God, the source of all truth.

The Way We Are

As we study American society today, we see that it is made up of basically four groups of people who share similar characteristics and interests. We can therefore fit most of our population of people into the four groups established earlier: Builders, Boomers, Busters and Bridgers (or mosaics). As generations move through time, it causes a generational wave (or change). As the groups move along, it creates changes that are identified specifically with this generation. The larger the generation, the larger the change it creates.

Ever since the beginning of the last century, Americans have been fond of labeling things or groups of people that influence our culture. [26]

The Builder Wave (Change)

Many call it the GI or Gung-ho generation because of World War II:

- They were born between 1927 and 1945.
- Builders were characterized by their loyalty, faithfulness, and commitment.
- They will not give up their traditions or give in to radical change.
- They've worked their whole life for what they have and see no need to change, especially when you don't recognize the need for change.
- They can't see change for the unfamiliar alternatives.
- They don't want to accept the new ways of experiencing and learning about God.
- In fact, there is not much that most of them will change in terms of values, perceptions, and behaviors at this advanced state of life.

- Influential personalities in this group include Billy Graham, Martin Luther King Jr., Oral Roberts, Jimmy Carter, George Bush, John F. Kennedy, Ronald Reagan, Lena Horne, Jerry Falwell, Colin Powell, and those in your area.

Listen to the builder talk about the church: I've been a member here for fifty five years. My wife and I were born and raised right here in Bethel Church. Our children grew up right here in this church. They are all grown and gone now scattered all over the country. Accept for funerals we seldom get to see them! They are so *independent,* of course that's good because it helps them to handle life. Although her children are heading toward their forties and fifties it's hard on their mother because she rarely get to see them. They married fifty one years ago. He retired from the town water department after thirty years.

Longevity is all important to them: the same spouse, same church, same community, same friends, same vacation spot, same telephone company, they've enjoyed the same everything for the past fifty years. They were born before television.

Familiarity and predictability bring them a sense of comfort and success. I think all this change is why people are so dissatisfied with life and this country today. How can they enjoy life when they spend all the time trying to change it? The church is a place where changes often do more harm than good. It's just not good! You read the Bible and you'll see Jesus didn't spend all His time trying to get people into politics. Well I've tried so I'll have to leave it in God's hands and hope for the best.

The Boomer Wave (Change).

The Boomer generation is the largest and most studied generation in U. S. history. It comprises two major groups: the Leading-Edge Boomers (LEBs) and the Trailing-Edge Boomers (TREBs). Influential members of this group include Spike Lee, Oprah Winfrey, George W. Bush, and Sylvester Stallone.

- They were born between 1946 and 1964.
- They are action-centered people.
- They are growth-centered.
- They have a reputation for being rebellious, affluent, and *independent.*
- They have lived during a strong economy.
- They vividly remember the Vietnam War.
- They cannot imagine the world without TV.

Listen to the Boomer talk about church: "It took marriage and a baby to get me here. I pretty much quit the church when I left for college and never saw a reason to go back. Of course my wife and children changed that, and for the kids, I think it turned out to be a pretty good decision." Today Joe is the assistant superintendent in the city school system. He was a teacher assistant for five years as he completed a Bachelor of science Degree. After spending several years in the classroom, he completed his Master Degree. He rapidly moved up the ladder as a principal, jumping from school to school every couple of years as better offers came along, until his status in the most prestigious school in the city; which landed him in his present position. He has his doctorate and soon the superintendent will be retiring. He solved the long-running battle with his wife about church and gave in. He joined the church, but to him it's just a remnant from a by-gone era. Actually he is bored with all of these non-professional people.

Of course I won't complain too much at least the pressure of competition and professionalism is off here. One thing I found out Church politics is just as bad and brutal as vying for schools. Joe admits some of the people are the nicest people in the world. I'm happy for the kids and I really do like the church's focus on spiritual things. Here I am a professional educator on my way up and they stick me on a committee that hasn't accomplished a thing in the last three years; it just meets and meets and meets. I finally figured it out I'll never be a leader in this church because real leaders threaten the pastor. You talk about updating things and you see another side of those guys. Those old-timers hate change. If it wasn't for my wife I would have left years ago. Another issue is the facilities. There's always some kind of building or renovation program going on that requires us to "give above and beyond." When the kids grow up and go to college there's going to be some changes made and this church is going to top the list. This church is going to have to compete if they want to get along with me. All this antiquated stuff. Take the music, why should I have to listen to choirs and organs? I've got to sit through the irrelevant stuff and that upsets me.

Since boomers are people, experience, and growth oriented, churches must be less concerned with programs and be more concerned with the needs of people. And since boomers are action-oriented, churches must do rather than just discuss. Author Mike Bellah warns us that "the baby boom is simply too big and too influential to be ignored. Industries have been made or broken by the boom. Businesses have learned the hard way that you neglect the baby boomer at your own peril. [27] Churches that want to grow should pay close attention as the boomers are now retiring, so churches would do well not to ignore them but adjust their ministries to attract and keep them.

The Buster Wave (Change)

The Buster generation was born between 1965 and 1983. Influential people of this group include and Johnny Depp, and Winona Ryder. Now in their thirties and forties, Busters:

- May be the most abused, forgotten, and alienated generation of the four.
- They have experienced a fluctuating economy.
- Desert Storm and MTV.

Listen to the Buster talk about church: Jimmy is thirty years old mired in a town with a college degree and no career goals; he is currently involved in car sales. He single, and says he want to travel around the world from city to city. He has saved no money to make that goal a reality. He lives a forty minutes' drive from his mother; which to him is ideal, close enough for quick meals and laundry, but far enough to maximize his *independence*.

He was raised in a Methodist church. After about twelve years of weekly attendance his parents suddenly divorced. His mother took him and two younger siblings and moved into a smaller house in a different community and stopped going to church altogether. "Mom had to drop unnecessary things and go into a survival mode. Her world shrunk to only focusing on what was important to survival. Church was not one of the things she felt she needed to survive. "That made an impression on me."

Today religion remains a major issue in his life. "I don't have a real strong church affiliation, but I'm pretty religious. I read a lot of stuff about religion, and my friends and I often talk about our beliefs and how religion affects our lives. I attend several different places, a Baptist church, Christian Science church, Methodist church and a non-denominational church. One of my friends is into Chrislam. Basically I'm a Christian but all the different churches put a spin on religion, which broadens my thinking and helps me to clarify what I really believe and to get what I really need." [28]

The Bridger or Mosaic Wave (Change)

The Bridger or Mosaic generation was born between 1984 and 2002. These young people do not want to be defined by a "normal" lifestyle. They favor a unique and personal journey. Many don't expect to get married or to begin a family as a young adult (if at all), though this may have been the expectation in the past. For mosaics:

- Relationships are the driving force.
- Being loyal to friends is one of their highest values.
- They have a strong need to belong, usually to a tribe of other loyal people who know them well and appreciate them.
- Still under their relational connectedness lies fierce *individualism*.

- Though they esteem fair-mindedness and diversity, they are irreverent and blunt.
- Finding ways to express themselves and their rage is an endless pursuit.
- Being skeptical of leaders, products, and institutions is part of their generational coding with extreme self-confidence.
- They do not trust things that seem too perfect, accepting that life comes with its share of messiness and off-the-wall experiences and people.
- Americans of all ages are inundated with media and entertainment options. Yet mosaics and busters consume many more hours of media from these sources than do older generations.
- Many enjoy immensely the latest hot movie, music, website, or pop culture buzz.
- Technologies connect young people to information and each other, and power their self-expression and creativity in ways older adults do not fully appreciate.
- Young people engage in a nearly constant search for fresh experiences and new sources of motivation.
- They want to try things out themselves, disdaining self-proclaimed experts and "talking heads" presentations.
- If something doesn't work for them, or if they are not permitted to participate in the process, they quickly move on to something that grabs them.
- They prefer casual and comfortable to stuffy and stilted.
- They view life in a nonlinear, chaotic way, which means they don't mind contradiction and ambiguity.
- They may tell someone what that person wants to hear, but then do whatever they desire.[29]

Listen to the Bridger / Mosaic talk about church: Spirituality is important but many consider it just one element of a successful, eclectic life. Fewer than one out of ten young adults mention faith as their top priority, despite the fact that the vast majority of Busters and Mosaics attended a Christian church during their high school years.

Most young people who were involved in a church as a teenager disengage from church life and often from Christianity at some point during early adulthood, creating a deficit of young talent, energy, and leadership in many congregations. While this is not uniquely Buster or Mosaic phenomenon, many Boomers did this too, however, Barna research suggests that today young people are less likely to return to the church later, even when they become parents.[30]

Let's look at a few statistics from a 2011 survey of some 18-29 year olds young people from Christian homes. This survey reveals some negative perceptions held by the bridgers about the institutional church:

- One out of five young people (21%) with a Christian background said, "I am a Christian, but the institutional church is a difficult place for me to live out my faith."
- One out of every eight young Christians (13%) said they "used to work at a church and became disillusioned."
- More than one-third of young Christians (38%) "want to find a way of following Jesus that connects with the world I live in."
- One-fifth (22%) want to "do more than get together once a week for worship.
- One-third (36%) agree that "I don't feel that I can ask my most pressing life questions in church."
- One out of ten (10%) put it more bluntly "I am not allowed to talk about my doubts in church."

This statistic signals one of the challenges that the next generation of Christians brings to the church. They are used to "having a say" in everything related to their lives. As Kinnaman noted earlier, fueled by technology is moving from passive to interactive. Yet the structure of young adult development in most churches and parishes is classroom-style instruction.

Leading a Church of Missionaries

Viewing the last section concerning the four generations, it's obvious that we must immediately take action while there is still hope for obeying our Christ-given mission of making disciples. The overarching problems seem to be:

1. Relying on antiquated strategies to keep the life's blood flowing in the local Churches [evangelism].
2. Little or no emphasis on sanctification [spiritual formation].
3. It is critical for the changing church that we *not* teach that discipleship is simply a set of things to do. Otherwise discipleship becomes work-centered and leads to legalism.
4. If we are anxious to be disciples of Jesus, then we must be in right relationship with Him.
5. Practicing His presence through prayer puts life and wisdom into our efforts as we ask the Spirit's help.
6. In retrospect, I think we should answer the question, what is a disciple?
7. A disciple is a pupil, an apprentice. It also means "to be or become a pupil or disciple." It is our mission to make disciples of Jesus (Matthew 28:19) and the word disciple means to be a student, pupil, or apprentice of Jesus, how will we approach this role in the changing culture and diversity of generations?

While memorizing Scriptural verses or reading study pamphlets and books are good and necessary; we don't want to miss the whole point. We must remember these are only means. The Holy Spirit is the one who changes, grows, and sanctifies us (study Romans 6-8).

Many Christians have been good at *sitting* around trying to perfect their doctrine, but few seem to make the connection of obeying Jesus' command to go into the world and make disciples of all nations. Are we playing with God? Too many Christians want people to think that they are pious, when in reality they are living in disobedience and deception. We will experience true Christian unity, when our eyes are on the Great commission. The Scripture declares, "The reason the Son of God appeared was to destroy the works of Satan" (1 John 3:8).

To affect meaningful strategies for making disciples, we must first stop settling for programs and events that only reap tiredness (pass out tracts, meetings at church, the means become the ends) and legalism (learn to adhere to a system of rules and steps). Rather, we must be disciples of Jesus who are dependent on the Holy Spirit to transform us into people who love God with all our heart and who loves people so much that we cannot help but be mission-minded 24/7. Disciples of Jesus are those learning to be like Him. This is the whole process of sanctification. Sanctification is our spiritual formation as the Spirit of God shapes and forms us from the inside out.

In Hebrews 6:1-3, the author admonishes the readers of his letter to leave the basics and go on to perfection, meaning "maturity." He lists six items in three couplets that he calls *the elementary principles of Christ:*

1. *Repentance from dead works*—refers to a change of mind about the demands of the Law of Moses (9:14). Even though the Law was good (see 1 Timothy 1:8), it was weak because of the weakness of our sinful nature (see Romans 8:3).
2. *Faith directed toward God*—not lifeless works that cannot save.
3. *Baptisms*—refer to the various baptisms in the New Testament [the baptism of Christ, of John, of believers, and the spiritual baptism of the believers], or to the various ritual washings practiced by the Jewish people.

4. *Laying on of hands*—in the Book of Acts, it was used to impart the Holy Spirit (see Acts 8:17, 18; 19:6). It was also used for ordination for ministry (see Acts 6:6; 13:3).

5. *Resurrection of the dead*—refers to the resurrection of all people at the end of time (Revelation 20:11-15). To Christians, belief in the bodily resurrection of Jesus was essential, for without His resurrection there is no forgiviness of sin (see 1 Corinthians 15:12-17).

6. *Eternal judgment*—refers to the belief that everyone will be judged by the great Judge. The Scriptures indicate that there are two judgments; one for believers in which Jesus determines every believer's reward (see 1 Corinthians 3:12-15), and the other judgment of condemnation on unbelievers (Revelation 20:11-20).

The six elements above take us back to that which is written in Hebrews 5:11-14, where the writer rebukes the Hebrews for their spiritual laziness and compared them to children taking milk when they should have been eating meat. They still needed some one to teach them when they should have been teaching others. These six items are the *first principles* which are the elements out of which everything develops.[31]

Keeping these first principles in mind we should evaluate everything we do in our churches by how the activity is producing mission-minded disciples. Everything should be thought of in this way. Everything:

- How are these classes guiding people toward being mission-minded?
- How does this sermon lead people to be mission-minded?
- In what ways do we see God using this event to build mission-minded disciples?
- Is intergenerational communications geared to build mission-minded disciples?

Generation Connections

Remember those who rule over you, **who have spoke the word of God to you,** *whose* **faith** *follow, considering the outcome of their* **conduct** (Hebrews 13:7). Three times in this chapter that guidance is given concerning *"them which have the rule over you."* [Emphasis mine]

1. In verse 7 they are to be *remembered.*
2. In verse 17 they are to be *obeyed.*
3. In verse 24 they are to be *saluted.*

The fact that "they have rule over us" signifies that they are leaders, those who guide us. However, this does not signify such spiritual superiority as some men and women declare today. It simply means that we are to recognize the fact that God appoints, pastors, teachers, and overseers of His flock.

Notice the Holy Spirit spells out that these leaders are to be those *"who have spoken the word of God to you."* Men and women anointed and appointed by God as channels through which His Word flows. We are not to salute them for their own sake, but for their works sake. It is what and whom they represent that demands our respect. These are people who live godly lives and we can follow their faith and their example. The church desperately needs more people who embrace a deeper vision of the authentic Christ, and the Christian faith in our pluralistic, and sophisticated culture.

We are at a turning point for authentic Christianity in this nation; and we must grasp these realities and respond in appropriate godly ways, as Christians, we are widely mistrusted by a skeptical generation. We have in church today godly senior men and women of faith and a generation of young people who are craving someone to mentor them, someone who will invest in their lives and show them the ways of the Lord. It seems that our churches are doing everything they can to keep these generations apart. The future of our churches hangs on the passing of faith from one generation to another through mentoring and intergenerational dialogue.

Many churches put a lot of time and energy into ministry to their elderly saints, sponsoring tours, planning fun outings, and pastoral care. Though all of this is appreciated, if not careful the church can overlook the seniors' most important need and that is simply to be needed. Despite what some may believe, people in the rising generations *deeply desire older spiritual mentors who will guide them in spiritual formation into a deeper life walking with Jesus.* World traveler Evelyn Christenson states that teens and those in their twenties feel that there's a gap here, where parents have really abandoned them and almost abdicated their responsibility in modeling and teaching biblical values. Some believe their parents left them unequipped as they sought "the good life." So these young people are looking to the elders in the church for the solid moral and spiritual footing they missed.[32]

Read in 2 Timothy 1:3-5 how Timothy's grandmother shared her faith down the generations. Titus 2:3-4, Psalm 71:18 and Joel 1:2-3 show how older generations were to impart the faith to younger generations. Despite obvious cultural differences, emerging generations have a deep longing for connection with and guidance from those who have wisdom and experience beyond their own. We must do whatever we can to encourage these mentoring relationships. We spend so much energy to encourage generations to worship together.

A mentoring ministry in which smaller groups of individuals can be matched with those who are older is a great way to accomplish this. If your church is mainly young people, consider establishing a relationship with another church of mainly older people. This would benefit both. Whatever it takes, the emerging church must work to establish mentoring relationships between older and younger generations. The passing on of wisdom must become a part of the emerging church today.

STUDY SUMMARY

CHAPTER 20

IT'S A DIFFERENT WORLD (VIEW)

According to Barna research, a new mode of thinking has emerged among young people.

A new mode of thinking in which linear reasoning [resembling a line, long and narrow] has been replaced with mosaic thinking, which integrates information and decision making in entirely.

The Scriptures take the theme of generations seriously; it affirms the different natures of generations, particularly that:

- Some generations are passive.
- Some generations are more responsive to the gospel than others.
- "A generation goes and a generation comes, but the earth remains forever" (see Eccles. 1:4).

There are four groups of people with shared characteristics. Those who range in ages:

- Late fifties and up are called builders.
- Late thirties to mid fifties are called boomers.
- The twenties to the mid thirties are called busters.
- Those younger than twenty are called Bridgers.

What was Jesus' stated reason for coming into the world?

Jesus came to destroy the works of Satan.

SOMETHING TO PONDER

After that whole generation had been gathered to their
fathers, another generation grew up, who knew neither
the Lord nor what He had done for Israel—Judges 2:10.

Train up a child in the way that he should go and when he
[or she] is old he will not depart from it—Proverbs 22:6.

Children are a gift from the Lord (most loved—most abused);
therefore we see our purpose in pondering children. We are seeing
the fruit of our handiwork at child-rearing. Are we proud or
ashamed? The increasing crime rates, greed, recent voting, decrease
in meaningful church attendance, and the downward spiral of the
culture; without a doubt indicate a change in the way we think (our
worldview), which are drastically affecting the local churches.

In the last section I stated that life-habits are established in
children at about five years old, that being true then at least by that
age parental influence toward Christ and the things of God, and a
viable Biblical world view should already be in place.

AIM: Develop a "truthful" Biblical worldview.

Proverbs 22:6 is one of the most misinterpreted passages
in Scripture. It may be the result of spiritual ignorance, or a
number of other reasons. However, in that one little verse there
is enough saving grace to save and set all children on the path of
righteousness for life. That truth lies in the promise that God made
here, it's linked to a command:

1. The command—"Train up a child in the way he [or she] should go!" (Parental responsibility).
2. The promise—"When he [or she] is old he [or she] *will not* depart from it." (God's responsibility).
3. We have a tendency to embrace the promise, but ignore the command.

What does it mean to train up a child? Let's prayerfully explain the meaning by expounding on three points:

Lead the child to Christ.

- Salvation is basic. Expecting a child to live a Christian life when he or she doesn't possess that life is ludicrous.
- You can't expect the child to fly; when he or she has no wings. The Christian life is not just difficult. It is impossible!
- The Christian life is supernatural life and not until the Holy Spirit takes up residence in a heart can a person live a life that pleases God. Many people acknowledge God and that is good but we must go on to knowing Him, personally. We must plant the truths of God's Word into that young, tender heart. Faith comes by hearing the Word of God. Tell them God's story, beginning in Genesis. It's so easy for parents to get caught up with sharing their faith with others outside of the home and neglect your own inside the home. Notice the biblical illustration:

"But as for you, continue to hold to the things that you have learned and of which you are convinced, knowing from whom you learned [them]. And how from your childhood you have had a knowledge of and been acquainted with the sacred Writings, which are able to instruct you and give the understanding for salvation which comes through faith in Christ Jesus [through the leaning of the entire human personality on God in Christ Jesus in absolute trust and confidence in his power, wisdom, and goodness] (2 Timothy 3:14-15 AMP.).

"I am calling up memories of your sincere and unqualified faith (the leaning of your entire personality on God in Christ in absolute trust and confidence in His power, wisdom, and goodness), [a faith] that first lived permanently in the heart of] your grandmother Lois and your mother Eunice and now, I am [fully] persuaded, [dwells] in you also" (2 Timothy 1:5). *". . . . I remember you day and night in my prayers"* (v. 3 AMP).

Notice the "principle of spiritual genetics." The apostle traces the linage of communication [chain of spiritual reproduction], that takes place beginning with the grandmother, and communicated to the mother, and now embraced by the child.

PERSONAL REFLECTIONS:

1.
2.
3.

"Train" or "Train up" (is used four times in the O.T.)

It means to "Dedicate"—which is the setting aside exclusively [the child] for God's purposes in his or her life.

- First by the reality in your own life.
- Second by teaching them the truth of the Gospel.
- This Scriptural foundation for life is our responsibility.

"Train" or "Train up" requires clear cut objectives. Many of us begin with great intentions, but what happens when the time comes to implement? This is not child's play!

This is the key verse to the Book of Proverbs, written from a parent to his child, Solomon to his son. The book covered areas he wanted to impact in his son. The book moves into such areas as:

- Parent and child relations
- Workplace relations
- Laziness and industry
- To be a thief or a liar
- To be known by truth
- How to relate to the opposite sex
- Sex education
- The dangers of materialism
- The tongue
- Wisdom
- Many are repeated over an over

The book is called *"The Parent's Manual for Child-rearing."*

List the five most important areas you would like to impact your children or grandchildren with [List in order of priority]. (Study Moses' example in Deuteronomy 6):

1.
2.
3.
4.
5.

The proper grading principle for the first grade is designed to be built upon in the second grade. *But you don't start teaching a child in the sixth grade!*

Start with the first basic twelve years of life of which the first five years are the formative years. Watch those sleepovers in homes you don't know!

We are characterized not by Christian standards, but by standards of Christians. Only biblical standards count. When children ask, "Why do we do this?" "Why don't we do that?" You have your convictions, but are they biblical?

Our children and even some of us have failed, because we were raised on second-hand standards. They were never our own. That will not fly in this post-Christian society.

PERSONAL REFLECTIONS:

1.
2.
3.

Be a Consistent Example

People don't want you to lecture them, but we've got to speak up. Of course let us not forget you are already communicating by your conduct and behavior in your own life.

- Many people are known by what they don't do (List the worldliness that comes to mind).
- Tell me what you are doing, that are the (marks of Christlikeness).

Spiritually speaking what are you known for? Are you noted for being that person that is always helpful in your church, known for your love, for your thoughtfulness, or your interest in others? Can you explain your remarks and actions biblically?

MY LIFE APPLICATION

1.
2.
3.

A CHARGE TO KEEP I HAVE

A charge to keep I have, A God to glorify,
Who gave His Son my soul to save,
And fit it for the sky.
To serve the present age,
My calling to fulfill,
O may it all my pow'rs engage
To do my Master's will.
Arm me with jealous care,
As in thy sight to live,
And O thy servant prepare
A strict account to give.
Help me to watch and pray,
And on Thy-self rely,
By faith assured I will obey,
For I shall never die.

—**Charles Wesley**

END NOTES

Introduction

[1]   Joshua Lingel, Jeff Morton and Bill Nikides, *Chrislam: How Missionaries Are Promoting an Islamized Gospel,* (i2 Ministries Publishing, 2011). iii.

Chapter 1: God's Eternal Story

[2]   S. Michael Craven, *Uncompromised Faith,* (Navpress, the publishing ministry of Navigators, 2009). 43.

Chapter 6: His Blood For Our Sins

[3]   Derek Prince, *God's Word Heals,* (Derek Prince Ministries-International, 2010).

[4]   Warren W. Wiersbe, *Wiersbe's Expository Outlines of the New Testament* (Chariot Victor Publishing, 1992). 426.

Chapter 15: Unity in the Church

[5]   Chic-fil-A: *Who We Are,* www. Chic-fil-A.com (accessed 14 January 2013).

[6]   C. Peter Wagner, *Changing Church,* (Published by Regal Books, 2004). 183.

[7]   Sam Walton, *Made in America,* (Doubleday, 1992). 249.

[8]   1 John 2:19

[9]   Warren W. Wiersbe, *Wiersbe's Expository Outlines of the New Testament* (Chariot Victor Publishing, 1992). 405.

10   Henry Drummond, *The Greatest Thing in the World* (Fleming H. Revell Company). 24.
11   Ibid. 27.
12   Alpha-Omega Ministries, Inc. *The Teacher's Outline & Study Bible [Ephesians]* (Leadership Ministries Worldwide Publishing 1996). 43.
13   Ray C. Stedman, *Body Life,* (Discovery House Publishers, Revised edition by Elaine Stedman, 1995). 15.

Chapter 19: By My Spirit said the Lord

14   A noted metaphor in Paul's writings to the Corinthians is "the body of Christ" (1 Corinthians 12:13).
15   Ray Bakke, *The Urban Christian: Effective Ministry in Today's Union World* (Downers Grove, IL: InterVarsity Press, 1987), 57.
16   Ibid.
17   John M. Perkins, ed., *Resorting At-Risk Communities: Doing It Together and Doing It Right* (Grand Rapids, MI: Baker Books, 1995), 12.
18   Mark A. Noll, *A History of Christianity in the United States and Canada* (Grand Rapids, MI: Eerdmans Publishing, 1992), 386.
19   Vinson Synan, General Editor, *Spirit-empowered Christianity in the 21st Century* (Charisma House Publishing, 2011) 478.
20   Ibid.

Chapter 20: It's a Different World (View)

21   Gary L. McIntosh, *One Church, Four Generations* (Baker Books Publishing, Grand Rapids MI. 2002) 10.
22   George Barna, *The Second Coming of the Church* (Word Publishing, a unit of Thomas Nelson, Inc. Nashville, TN. 1998) 4.
23   Gary L. McIntosh, *One Church, Four Generations* (Baker Books Publishing, Grand Rapids, MI. (2002) 198.
24   Ibid.15.
25   S. Michael Craven, *Uncompromised Faith* (Navpress publishing, Colorado Springs, CO. (2009) 20.
26   Ibid. Adapted. 16.

27 Mike Bellah, *Baby Boom Believers* (Wheaton: Tyndale House, 1988), 129.

28 Adapted from George Barna, *The Second Coming of the Church,* Word Publishing, Nashville, TN. (1998). 72.

29 David Kinnaman, *Un Christian,* Published by Baker Books, Grand Rapids, MI. (2007). 21.

30 Ibid. 23.

31 Hebrews 5:11-14; 6:1-3

32 Dwight Perry, *Building Unity in the Church of the New Millennium:* An edited interview with Evelyn Christenson, *Is There a Place for Elderly Saints in the Body of Christ"*(Moody Press, 2002). 263.